Table of Contents

Introduction 1

Chapter 1: What Are Morals? 5

Chapter 2: How Can I Be A Good Person? 17

Chapter 3: Living By The Golden Rule 27

Chapter 4: The Key To Being A Moral Person 34

Chapter 5: Morality and religion 50

Chapter 6: What is Amorality? 56

Chapter 7: Morality And Ethics In Society Today 66

Chapter 8: The Laws Of Nature 76

Chapter 9: Morality And Justice 89

Chapter 10: Ethical Theories 100

Chapter 11: How To Grow Spiritually And Morally 114

Introduction

"Morality is the basis for the ethics we possess in society today and everything that we believe and strive to believe in. We as a society struggle morally yet everything we should aim to do is for the greater good. Everything we fight for should be based on anything that we commit to be morally sound and superior in ethical nature and goodness."

Morality is a unique and complex system of beliefs and ethical ideas that we tend to live by on a day-to-day basis, yet usually don't give much thought about. Morality has been a life-long battle for many people out there and in society today. In every society you'll find a different set of moral beliefs across cultures, through societies, and throughout time periods. It's important that we learn about the concepts of morality so we can better ourselves, our loved ones, and spread love light harmony and the concept of truth, goodness, and true morality to others out there and make the world an even better and greater place than it is. The concepts in this book will allow you to expand your mind, grow your consciousness and awareness and be able to harness and increase your own moral levels and become better people who live happier more fulfilled lives.

Do you know how to be a moral person? Do you feel you are a good person, or do you often wonder whether you're not as good of a person as you thought you were? Morals play a key role in developing who you are as a person and your entire make-up and can affect your existence in a major way. You are what you believe in, how you think, act, speak, your very actions and intent make up everything regarding the person that you are. You are a living being and every part of you breathes a thought within yourself. Your ethical principles are an integral part of you and are the key to your success and further developing yourself as a person. Do you hold strong moral beliefs about life, religion, goodness, and evil or do you rarely think about these things?

It is okay either way- for you can begin to ponder upon that which is moral or immoral, good versus bad and the conflicts of evil in our society. Being an ethical person doesn't take perfection, it only takes the knowing and understanding, the realization of awareness and intent, and the good intentions that a person can possess to expand their wonderful awareness and grow to knowing more about themselves, becoming greater moral and spiritual people, and harnessing their newfound lessons to help and teach others.

Your life matters, and the foundations for your moral beliefs are an integral part of society today. Every person's actions, words, and thoughts count towards the collective whole and we need to learn how to harness that awareness and grow into becoming greater and more moral human beings in general and spreading that which is goodness love and light and even eliminating that which isn't beneficial to others, ourselves and society or which might be harmful.

This book will allow you to expand your knowledge and awareness of the principles that exist in today's society which shape our belief systems and how we perceive life and anything in this world. You can and will grow and increase your level of morality and learn to become a better, more vibrant, good, positive, and greater person than you used to be.

Do you feel you live by morals on a day-to-day basis, or do you not fully grasp the concept of morality? Do you feel as if you are a noble or moral person or are these thoughts you don't think of too often? Take no heed, you're definitely not the only one! Not a large number of people harbor daily thoughts about the actions they perform, the feats they accomplish, or ponder upon whether they are good people or not. That is because most people don't come across circumstances which cause them to contemplate this very subject. Most people are too busy with their own lives, the caveats of everyday living, and life's up and downs to focus on the status of their own levels of morality on a daily basis.

The concept of morality dates back to ancient times, where the Greeks and Germans helped coin the term, but it is something we should strive towards and think about a lot more often than usual.

Morals are a great part of our daily lives whether we believe or think about them or not. We often fail to contemplate our daily lives, our actions, and our intent. The Moral Journey will allow you to contemplate the concept of morality, teach you what morality is, and allow you to expand your mind and increase your knowledge and awareness regarding the concept of righteousness and morals overall.

If you have always wondered whether you were a good person or not, look no further, you can develop that question and examine it and the many lessons that you will discover. You will expand your mind, increase your awareness, and gain a better understanding of the concept of ethics than you previously had as well as grow in morality and gain better virtues than you had before.

CHAPTER 1

What Are Morals?

"The most important human endeavor is the striving for morality in our actions. Our inner balance and even our very existence depend on it. Only morality in our actions can give beauty and dignity to life."
-Albert Einstein

Morals are the rules that we live by, and the way we encompass our daily lives and the rules that we abide by while we are existing here on this beautiful planet. Morality can date back to ancient times and each society had their own sets of laws and rules. We can easily understand how these rules and standards are governed by their own societies and it's important to understand the concept of how morals came about.

The word moral comes from the Latin term Moralis, which means pertaining to manners and morality began around 400,000 years ago, when people began hunting and gathering events. Most notions of morality have been formed through a combination of our genes and culture together. The concept of morals is generally formed throughout a person's life starting at a very young age and people's beliefs are generally molded by their parents, their upbringing, the society they come from, and their culture and genetic makeup.

True morality is about upholding and the keeping up of great tradition which is about upholding the laws of your society and nature, but more so by the great laws and rules which govern the whole of any society. These laws and rules stem from the concept of good versus bad, and right versus wrong, and are generalized in most cases by the claims that actions such as murder, theft, or most wrongdoings of any nature are against moral code and are known as crimes that can or will be punishable in various forms.

True morality stems from the concept of being an exemplary person and citizen in your own world, society and territory. There are of course many different ways of upholding the standards of morality and decency. The basis of being a moral person and holding ideations that are similar throughout cultures involves concepts such as goodness, honesty, justice, fairness, being humble and not arrogant. There are many other concepts and qualities a person can behold that can constitute the ideation of true morality within a person.

The moral code is a set of principles or rules that typically rule as a guide for people's behavior, allowing them to determine the difference between right and wrong. It can be a guide for ethical decision-making and helps shape a person's moral values and beliefs. There are many common moral principles that most people are taught to live by- some of these include being an honest person, fairness, justice, compassion and doing good unto others rather than harm.

The moral code that a person lives by is molded and created by their upbringing, and by many other facets and factors in their life these things are actually assisted by several different factors, and the concept of morality, stems from a person being able to live by their own rules and laws, that are founded in their own society.

Culture plays a significant role in shaping morality as it provides the norms, values, and beliefs that influence how individuals perceive and evaluate moral issues. Cultural practices, traditions, and social norms can vary across different societies leading to differences in moral standards and judgments.

How do you personally feel about morality? Do you feel as if you are a moral person, or do you feel as if you have little concept of the idea between right and wrong? Do you know the difference between right and wrong and good versus bad or do you not think about these things in your daily life? It is extremely important that you as a human being harness an awareness of the concept of morality, rather than ignoring the fact that this idea exists in the world. It is extremely important for each and every individual to focus on morals and focus on doing good deeds and actions, and being people that abide by specific kinds of moral values that exist on this planet, and in society itself. It's extremely important to be aware of the concept of morality, the concept of living a specific way, and to be aware of our deeds, and what we do on this planet, rather than being in the dark and having no knowledge of these things.

Do you feel as if morality just doesn't exist, or do you not think about these things on a day-to-day basis? Well, if you answered no to this question, you are not in the minority. Most people don't have a solid moral code they abide by though there are a large number of people that actually do.

Moral codes can exist within societies, and these specifically also exist within religious texts, and these religious texts have specific moral codes that a person must abide and live by. Religious texts and belief systems hold very strict moral laws and values that they teach societies to live by and are very staunch when it comes to upholding these belief systems. They teach the world and society the manner in which we should live by, and the very means by which we should uphold these practices and belief systems in order to live moral and good lives and so we can sustain these laws.

Morals are the ethics we must live and abide by in order to live in a sound and civilized society in today's world. The morals we uphold and live by are an extremely important means for us to live a decent honest and virtuous reality as opposed to one that doesn't contain the concept of morals guiding it in some form.

Morals influence society in a huge way. They shape societal norms, values, behavior, and they assist with cooperation, empathy and bringing people together. They do influence the laws, and policies and allow a more just and ethical society. We are heavily influenced by those around us including society, culture, what we watch on tv, movies, music, media, social media, and many other aspects in general. Most people have gotten lost in the influence of all of these other ideations in life, rather than allowing morals, religion, or ethics to influence them in a bigger way. It is important that we get influenced by anything that is of benefit and very positive and helpful to us and within our lives and world rather than anything that might be of harm. The influence of morality in our lives can be of great benefit and it's something we should strive towards more often.

Morality is about the principles and standards that we possess concerning right versus wrong behavior, and it's about guiding people into making ethical or wise decisions. It also involves the idea of fairness, justice, and goodness and the concepts of doing that which is good or just as opposed to doing something of an ill nature.

True morality is rooted in complete and utter goodness and the doing of only good and against all that which is evil, harmful, or not beneficial to life or humanity in general. It's important to live by these specific rules and focus on doing all that is harmless and good and beneficial to others and straying from anything that might be harmful in nature to others and to us as well.

There are several stages of moral development that have been studied and recognized by psychotherapists. Psychologists have categorized these stages as the pre-conventional stage, the conventional stage, and the post-conventional stage. Kohlberg, a psychologist developed these stages of moral development and has established them since 1958. After presenting people with different moral dilemmas, Kohlberg categorized their responses into different stages of moral reasoning.

Using children's responses to a series of moral dilemmas, Kohlberg established that the reasoning behind the decision was a greater indication of moral development than the actual answer.

Pre-conventional stage:

The pre-conventional stage of moral development generally lasts until a child is about eight years old. This is the first level of moral development and children accept the authority of those above, and the moral beliefs taught to them, until this age.

During this moral stage level, people tend to follow the rules or obey authority so they cannot get in trouble, or they want to get a specific reward. This is all based on what authority figures tell you to do, rather than you knowing or thinking what is right or wrong. Children usually make moral decisions based on the level of punishment involved or the consequences of the actions.

For example, if an action leads to punishment, it must be bad; if it leads to a reward, it must be good.

People at this pre-level don't have a sense of right or wrong just yet. They think that something is good if they get rewarded for it, or that something is bad if they get punished for it. It is similar to almost training an animal to receive treats for good behavior and to get scolded for negative behavior. At this level, moral decisions are shaped by the standards of adults and the consequences of following or breaking their rules.

The Conventional Stage

This is the adolescent stage of moral development focused in societal norms and external expectations to discern right from wrong, often grounded in tradition, cultural practices, or established codes of conduct.

The moral standards of valued adult role models at the conventional level are recognized and internalized. Authority is internalized but not questioned, and reasoning is based on the group's norms to which the person belongs.

So, people who follow conventional morality believe that it is important to follow society's rules and expectations to maintain order and prevent problems. An example is that cheating in gym glass can lead to an issue with the entire class and is socially looked down upon, so it's something that no one would do. During this level of moral development, the child often wants to be seen as a good person, therefore their moral actions relate to the approval of others. The child also becomes more aware of the moral rules affected by the laws of society and morality, so a lot of their moral actions stem from trying to upload societal laws and rules, and to avoid guilt.

Post-Conventional Stage:

Post conventional morality is the third level of moral development created by Arthur Kohlberg, and it's understood by its beliefs in universal ethical principles. Postconventional morality is when people decide based on what they think is right, rather than just following the rules of society. People at this last level or stage of morality have finally developed their own ethical principles and don't do what society tells them to do- they are able to come up with conclusions and beliefs of their own terms.

People tend to think about what is fair, just, and what values are most important. People also tend to think about how their choices and actions affect others and make good decisions for everyone and not just for themselves. Values include the preserving of life at all costs and the importance and value of human life, values, and dignity. Individual judgment is based on self-chosen principles, and moral reasoning is based on the rights and justice of each individual.

According to Kohlberg, this level of moral belief and reasoning is as far as people get. People at this stage have developed their own set of moral rules by which they live, which may or may not abide by the law. Other stages include situations where people are prepared to defend their principles even if it means going against the rest of society and having to pay the consequences. Kohlberg doubts that most people get to this stage and usually end at the third stage. There are some issues with Kohlberg's reasoning and the stages he created. The dilemmas can be construed as artificial, the research samples used are biased, the dilemmas are hypothetical, they aren't real, the research design is poorly done, and there is no real basis that there are stages of moral development that do exist.

The morals of people today

Hundreds of studies have shown and proven that the people of today's society feel that the morals of society are in general decline. The problem is that the perception of moral decline has been present throughout history and through time with people having the same perception as they do today. During the times of Jesus, people felt as if those were the 'end of times and days', and people have felt this way as well throughout the history of humanity. We often hear the phrase that things were better in the past than they are today, however, the problem is that this phrase has been heard and spoken throughout history and during each era, and the consensus seems to stay the same. An analysis of surveys conducted around the world since 1949 shows that the idea of a decline in moral values is omnipresent, whatever the social or historical context.

When asked about their own morality, four out of five Americans believe themselves to be moral people, while 12 percent believe themselves to be immoral. According to a recent poll, 54 percent of Americans feel the state of moral values in the country is poor, and 83 percent believe that the morals of people and society is in a steady decline. Data published from June 2023 show that people in general feel that people are less moral now than they used to be. The data was taken from a survey of more than 12 million people and shows that people have felt this way for 70 years. Societies in general feel that the moral state of humanity is in a general decline. Numerous people feel as if people are less ethical than they were before.

Are people really less honest, generous, decent, and more evil, spiteful, hateful, and full of negativity as compared to before and less moral in nature? This is an age-old question that has been studied for decades now. The truth of the matter is that morals really aren't in a huge decline the way people feel they are. There are psychologists who have studied the perception of moral decline in the world and during this era, and who feel that this concept of moral decline is nothing more than a perception and not something upon a basis that is true or founded.

Specific groups, such as homosexuals or people with disabilities, are treated better today than they were decades ago. Violent phenomena such as slavery, murder, rape, and massacres have declined over the last few centuries, but people still feel as if the concept of morals and morality on the planet have declined, yet this concept or belief is something that has held solid for decades and even centuries. People often feel that the moral decline of the world seems to have begun at the time of their birth and seems to get worse as they age, and as new generations come into existence.

There are psychologists who believe that there are two cognitive biases known as the negativity bias and the memory bias, which create this illusion that there is such a large mass of moral decline and phenomena in society today, when the truth is the opposite seems to be happening. The negativity bias refers to the fact that people pay more attention to negative media, attention, and data. People absorb and gather more negative than positive information about the current moral state of the world and conclude that it is low.

The second is memory bias. Our negative memories fade faster than our positive ones. The first bias makes the present world and society seem like it has huge moral issues, the second makes the past seem like a great moral universe", the study concludes. So now there is a moral dilemma going on due to the fact that people in general feel as if there is a decline in morals. People are going to feel less happy in general, more suspicious of others, and feel as if others just aren't as good as they used to be. This way of thinking, and distorted perception as many psychologists put it can have dire consequences for society as a whole and the way people interact with each other and people's beliefs in one another.

CHAPTER 2

How Can I Be A Good Person?

"Ethics is knowing the difference between what you have a right to do, and what is right to do" Potter Stewart

What is a good person?

It's hard for most people to understand exactly what makes up a good person or what entails being good, upstanding, or moral. We live in a confusing society where goodness can sometimes be mistaken for kindness or weakness. Being a good person is an integral part of being an upstanding citizen in the world and in society.

Being a moral person is an important part of existing on this planet and being a part of society and civilization. Now what exactly makes up a good person? You might actually be a very good person and ask yourself this very question. Am I a good person and what exactly makes up someone who is good? The answer to that is, you can do a lot of self-examination and introspection to attempt to figure out whether you are truly a moral person or not, or if you fall into the category of being somewhere in the negative version of the situation.

Being a good person is one of the most important aspects of existing in society though most people don't exactly perceive it this way. Morality isn't what it used to be nor are standards by which people uphold moral codes or ideals. In order to become a morally decent and good person, a person must abide by the basic standards and rules of morality and what is present in society. Society has standards by which a person can judge the basis of morality and these standards are the very basic concept of right versus wrong, and good versus evil.

Do you feel you're a good person? Or do you feel as if you're just not good enough to be considered an upstanding moral citizen of your society? Sometimes, the concept can be difficult to gauge. Most people for instance, feel as if they are just good people in general, however, not everyone can fit the bill for being a decent or good person when it comes to normal standards of morality or goodness.

The beauty of being a good person who is of a higher awareness is that you typically don't worry too much about what others think when it comes to what you believe in or how you feel about life in general. Then again you might say, well why can't a good person care about what others think about them? The truth of the matter is, there are plenty of good people who do care what others think about them and that doesn't mean they aren't good people. What is being referred to is more a level of a higher awareness that a particular kind of person possesses, and once someone has this level of awareness, and has the capability of being able to self-analyze themselves and learn exactly who or what they are and develop into truly good genuine people and hold this awareness, then they truly don't care what others think about them.

When a person possesses the standards of morality and true genuine goodness they usually are of a higher awareness, and they have a deeper understanding of life and everything that encompasses this world and where we exist. Again, it doesn't mean that if you don't grasp this higher awareness, you're not a good person. On the contrary- you can be an even better person than the person with the higher awareness, however most people who are truly genuinely good people are going to have some level of greater awareness and a level of greater compassion, for with the compassion and awareness they possess, comes a greater level of understanding and good within their own lives, reality and in the lives of others as well.

A truly good person doesn't worry about the thoughts of others and doesn't focus on the perception of others but more so on the perception of God, goodness, nature and their own selves and the things that matter in life.

Goodness and morality

Goodness and morality stem from many different factors including culture, upbringing, personal boundaries, and other things which have contributed to the development of the person. Goodness is the antithesis of evil, and we live in a society where evil has upheld its roots in most people's daily lives. The concept of evil tends to be prevalent in most people's minds and within their own souls and lives as well.

Now what does it truly take to be a good person, you might ask? This is a confusing question for most because it's complicated to know what entails a person to be good or who has this specific characteristic. You might think that being a good person encompasses having a specific quality, such as humbleness, lack of arrogance, wisdom, knowledge, morality, humility, and many other beneficial qualities that are positive or that are of benefit to others. Being a good person really does entail doing good deeds, and being a benefit to others and doing that which is harmonious and positive, rather than that which is negative or dark in any form.

Being a good person is about being extremely positive, and being of benefit to others, and wanting to help those out there rather than doing harm. We live in a society where, although people might be good in general, being a genuinely good person is something that is very scarce out there, due to the nature of what people have turned into.

Think of people in your life, your family, parents, siblings, friends-do you think or have daily thoughts about whether they are good people or are you just friends with them and interact with them on a normal basis? Do you often wonder about the true nature of their character or does that thought rarely or ever grace your mind. The problem is that most people lack higher awareness or an awareness, and they lack introspection, regarding those who are around them. They lack the concept of knowing the people within their lives, and analyzing or psychoanalyzing what type of people they are. You might be one of those people who does psychoanalyze the people around and sometimes ponders upon whether they are good people or not. In general, most people don't think this way-they don't tend to psychoanalyze and examine those who are their friends or family.

In general, are we good people-are we people that harness the qualities of goodness or are we people who actually have hints of evil and darkness within us? It is confusing to know what qualities people possess, and it's confusing to try to figure this out simply because we don't know every element of what a person is deep within themselves. However, it's also important to know that to be a good person you will want to eradicate and eliminate any dark areas that you might have within yourself and try to focus on being a person that is full of only positivity and goodness.

Do those who have hints or glimmers of evil or those who are capable of evil, possess the notion of being good people, or are these people considered more evil people than good people? It's difficult sometimes to determine who is good based on the level of ethics they possess within themselves or the levels of good and evil they harness or are capable of. There is also not the notion that if someone is better than evil, then they are considered to be good people, for those who hold evil within themselves, would have to be judged based on their actions, deeds, intentions, and their culpability for committing atrocities against another or the level or chance at which they would commit these actions.

True morality and goodness is rooted in eliminating all that is evil or harmful in one's life and in a person's interactions with others. In order to be a good person, you're going to want to do only good deeds and actions and focus on those good deeds and not doing that which is evil or harmful. There is a belief system that exists where people are against all that is harmful or evil and go only for that which is beneficial or good to others and to themselves as well. It is extremely important to follow this school of thought in order to be a truly good person and a better person overall. It is extremely important to act and live by the golden rule and do only good and decent acts to yourself and to others as well.

Practicing self-care is a very important part of being a good person and loving yourself and being good to and taking care of yourself. This of course, is not done in any selfish format. For many times, people often tend to forget about themselves, or even look down on themselves or are very hard on themselves for many different reasons. It's important to love yourself first and foremost and start from there and focus on grounding yourself and harnessing a vast amount of positive energy and being a good person from there on.

The key to being a good person has to do with the intent of a human deep within and even better, the notion inside the person that they strive and seek to do only good and gain pleasure and love from loving that which is good, noble, honest, decent and anything of good nature or of any form of good qualities. Enlightenment is the aftermath of being a creation that has been possessed or indoctrinated with the qualities of good or of love and light mostly or only in their body and souls. They embody only good, love and light and seek to spread that to others and want the cause and effect to incorporate only that which is positive or good.

As humans and intelligent beings, we should seek to do that only which is good, decent, or noble and as intelligent people with a fully developed mind and the concept of morality our usual way of thinking should revert to that which is pure and good only, not that which is evil, unfounded, or full of what isn't good. Being a good person and moral upstanding citizen and living being isn't always such an easy task. The problem is, everyone was born of innocence and beauty, love, and light. Babies and children are only of innocence and good and they don't think or feel evil thoughts or hold the capability of such things. They don't hold the culpability of right vs wrong and don't carry the notion of doing any form of evil or bad.

Things change for a person once they begin to grow and get older and develop their cognitive minds and the notion of good and evil begins to come into play. The concept of morality has to do with what we feel is right versus what we believe isn't right or what is wrong. Morals are the principles that guide individual conduct within society. Morals may change over time, yet they do remain the standards of behavior that we use to judge right and wrong.

While most people possess the notion of seeking to do good or doing good within them many people do not consciously strive to attain this characteristic or quality and aren't of the higher awareness to only be a good person and serve humanity in their own sense or do only good deeds and to go against that which isn't good. Being a Muslim, I grew up with a sense of right and wrong, but I learned a lot of my morals from the religion of Islam. I was constantly in a state of wanting to do the right thing but never being fully aware or conscious of this at all. Many people at a young age aren't aware of the notion of the higher awareness of right and wrong and the concept of true morality.

People in general may possess the idea of doing the right thing but simply don't possess the higher awareness or vision necessary in order to be fully aware of their actions or intent at times of performing tasks or doing things they generally do in their everyday lives. It's important to try to focus on those things that we know are good, decent moral or upright, rather than focusing on doing things or deeds that are immoral, selfish, or anything of negative value.

Being a spiritual person means that you need to focus on the inner part of you, the part that is your inner and deep soul and the part that seeks to be nourished by goodness, love light and beauty and that which possesses the ability of a greater growth than you can imagine if you only know how to aid this portion of yourself. Being an enlightened person comes from deep within the soul and in order to achieve that notion of enlightenment and goodness you must embrace that depth within your very core and soul, the light essence that seeks to illuminate you that which you cannot grasp or fathom due to it being concealed and hidden in your very core.

CHAPTER 3

LIVING BY THE GOLDEN RULE

"The most important human endeavour is striving for morality in our actions" -Albert Einstein

The Golden Rule

Living by the golden rule is a key element to living a moral and good life and reality on this planet today, though most of the principles of this law have been lost in the vast sea of disorientation that this society and our world have become. It seems like a simple rule to live by such as doing unto others and being a nice overall genuine person and not doing any kind of major harm to someone, however, this is not the situation that generally tends to occur in the society we're in today.

People have resorted to vast amounts of selfishness and greed, and they tend to not live by this very simple and ethical principle. People tend to live in a state of a lack of awareness and overall shallowness and a state of confusion and a true lack of introspection. One of the most important elements a person can possess is the concept of introspection.

This is because it's key to know and understand exactly how you feel and what you think as a human and what drives you specifically to do the things that you do. Sadly, most people are in a dilemma and fail to harness this concept of introspection and hardly ever examine their own thoughts and behaviors. Now what is introspection? Introspection is the examination or observation of one's own mental and emotional processes, and figuring out exactly who a person truly is and why they behave in the manner by which they commit the acts they do.

Living by the golden rule is something that we as humans and citizens of our society should be entitled to do on a regular basis in our daily lives. What exactly is the golden rule and why should we live by this or live in this way? Well, the golden rule particularly states that we need to do to others as we want to have done to us, but it's about equality and doing the right thing and doing good to others like we want good done to us as opposed to being evil or negative or doing any wrong deeds or wronging another human. We need to live our lives by treating others in the nicest and best way possible, because this will create harmony, and joy in our lives and throughout society as a whole, as opposed to something of the opposite that is chaos and disharmony.

The golden rule is the ethic of reciprocity, and this is a very important concept in today's society. You can find this rule present in cultures and religions throughout the world, including Islam, Christianity, Hinduism, Buddhism, and many other religions. The golden rule is a fundamental principle that focuses on the importance of treating others with respect, kindness, and compassion, and allows us to build greater relationships with others. It is the epic manner in which we should live our lives, and we should enjoy and yearn to live this way as well, for living in this way allows us to grow morally and lets us become better people in general and gain greater morals and ethics from practicing this way of life.

The golden rule originated from various cultures and religions. It can be found in ancient Egyptian, Greek, and Chinese texts, as well as in the teachings of many religious figures, including Jesus in the Bible and Confucius in Chinese philosophy.

In order to live by the golden rule, we need to be empathetic and kind gracious human beings and treat each other with respect and goodness. We need to be mindful of our own behaviors and practices with regards to how we behave towards others and to each other and even how we treat our own selves. We need to grasp what it's like to have a higher awareness and be cautious of our actions towards each other and live by being humbler, patient and kind human beings.

Our society is one where there is a large amount of greed and hatred and where people feel as if they are the center of their own worlds. The concept for this is known as egocentrism and people are ignorantly living through the lens of their own egos rather than the lens and beauty of being loving and giving people. There is a wonder and beauty with doing the right and best deeds and helping one another out, and this is the basis for how we should exist in this society.

Society and technology

You would think that we live in a civilized and highly technologized society. We are of course, living in the latest of modern times, however technology is what is the downfall of our current society. And we have somehow lost the beauty there once was of interacting with each other on a platonic and socially fun basis. Although people are social, they have lost the special nature of being interconnected with each other, the way things were decades and ages ago. People have become lost in their technology, their cell phones, social media, iPads, and have lost the beauty of positive fun interactions that used to occur in life and in society before technology became dominant in people's lives.

We feel as if things are perfect for us the way they are, but somewhere deep down we also know that things just aren't right most of the time. That is because, we've lost the basic concept of natural social interaction with each other, and we've lost the peace and harmony that came with being the social and happy people that we once were. Our society just isn't what it used to be, and we need to get back to the way things once were, though it may seem difficult to do so. Living by the golden rule and doing to others goodness and living with the concepts of kindness, decency, and mercy, we can revert back to old times when everything seemed different, and there was an overall genuineness and that doesn't seem to be as present these days as it was previously.

The basic concept of social interactions being mostly face-to-face or in person the way they were in the past just doesn't seem to be as dominant in today's society, where people find themselves stuck on their latest technological gadgets, losing the beauty and fun of genuine and heartfelt interactions. Phone calls have become replaced with texting, and one-on-one interactions can sometimes become lost in quick bursts of interactions, whereas in previous times, this just wasn't the case or something that was able to occur. Due to these scenarios and reasons, people aren't as social, positive, or genuine as they once were, and you'll find the concept of the golden rule and living by these ethics waning in society.

We live by the golden rule daily and typically tend to be nice, moral humble and upstanding people. Most people aren't generally evil people or would do deeds or things that go against that which is right or moral. However, a lot of the time our actions and deeds are done without much given thought, without the concept of introspection and without the notion of being aware of what exactly we're doing and without any given awareness or intent. It's important that we become mindful of the actions we commit only because with awareness comes change, and only then will we be able to live in true goodness and harmony not only with others, but with ourselves as well.

Once we're aware of our actions and deeds we can change our lifestyle and the way we think about life in general. Living by the golden rule can have a great impact on our lives, and it can turn us into happier, more positive, and better people in general. Once we're aware of our actions and our intent, and we enhance the awareness we have about ourselves and every action we partake in, then we can further grasp the concept of doing more good deeds and actions and living through the lens of doing good to others and having that good be returned to us.

Living by the golden rule is the beauty of the creed that it holds somewhere deep within the grasp of its understanding. If you truly love that which is good or moral, then you will enjoy and love the concept of doing good unto others and wanting that same good done not only to you, but to everyone and towards humanity as a whole. Those who are truly moral, good, decent, and upstanding human beings are the ones who are truly in love with that which is good, decent and noble and not that which is of the darkness or of negativity. If you love and enjoy living by the golden rule and truly seek to live by this concept with happiness and joy, then you're amongst the rare of the top good out there who think differently than most people.

For most people aren't exactly in love with doing and being a good person. They are in love with the world, material gains, worldly good and pleasures, and anything that doesn't represent character or something that isn't of material in nature. If you live by the golden rule, but take it even further by possessing an extra enjoyment and gift of love for that which is goodness, and doing good deeds, and having good intent with each action you partake in, you're taking it to the next level of being a truly good, decent and humble person and even a rare person in a world and society where it's rare to think on these terms.

CHAPTER 4

The Key To Being A Moral Person

What does being a moral person entail?

How can one determine who a good person is? Are you able to determine for yourself if you're truly a moral person? Have you ever practiced the art of self-analysis and attempted to figure out who you are inside and what your intent and actions have come to be? It can be difficult to attempt to define what measures one can use to figure out what makes up a good or bad person. Would you consider yourself to be a good person overall? Have you ever self-analyzed yourself or done any form of introspection? Do you feel you have good intent with the things you do in life, or do you not have very good intentions when it comes to doing things in general?

What characteristics define what or who a good person really is? Most people haven't taken the time to self-reflect or analyze exactly who they are, and they generally find themselves in varying states of depression, negativity and other forms of confusion that they don't fully comprehend or have a clue as to where it all stemmed from. It's important to know where your emotions are coming from and who exactly you are and why you commit the very acts you do commit. Once you understand your intent, then you can get a much better idea of what kind of person you are and why you do the acts or deeds that you do and the context in which these acts are committed.

A good person can possess an unlimited number of positive qualities and characteristics, or they can have a smaller number of these qualities as well and still be considered a person that can be categorized as 'good.' Of course, the term good is very subjective and is privy to every varying person but overall, there are specific attributes that can really make up what you may define as a good person.

The definition of 'good' can be described as something that is considered beneficial, positive or of a non-negative nature. It can be used to describe events, experiences, emotions, people, outcomes, or actions of others. The definition of good can also vary based on cultural and religious perspectives and can vary from society to society. The concept of good is also based on varying perspectives of each person and can be subjective to opinion, experience, and interpretation of each action or event. That's why it's just so hard to define what good actually is, though in reality the concept of good is going to be associated with that which is positive, helpful, or beneficial in some form.

The utilitarian theory of goodness states that actions are considered good if they maximize overall happiness or utility for many people at a given time. It also states that the consequences of any action are the only standard of right and wrong. It considers the interest of all humanity and sentient beings equally.

"We are the actions we commit, and we should do what we hope is done unto us"

Only do that which you would want done to you, otherwise you're contributing to the downfall of an already chaotic confused society. We are truly the actions and deeds that we commit. It is important to perform actions and acts that we want done to us back onto others, rather than the opposite.

Most humans are generally moral and decent people, yet this normally stems from the surface of who they are. Many humans tend to not be as moral or good as they feel they are because somewhere deep within their selves they do possess qualities of negativity or darkness, or these things are also present somewhere on the surface as well. It seems people in general tend to be good and decent moral people, yet reality sometimes shows people otherwise. Melissa seems to be a very nice female on the outside. She is polite, friendly, and gives her neighbors cookies every few months as a friendly gift since she is an excellent baker. However, somewhere within herself, Jennifer has some dark issues. She has a bad habit of smoking and whenever she gets a chance, she yells and gets angry at her daughter and takes her anger out on her sometimes due to her own internal issues. This doesn't mean that she isn't a good person, or a decent person who might have issues, it just means that she isn't the good-hearted gracious person that most people might think she is.

It is hard to define what a good person truly is only because people possess so many varying traits and characteristics within themselves. It's impossible to define what good is versus a bad person. There are ways, however, you can discern whether a person is good versus whether a person is mostly a bad person, and that is based on the actions and deeds they commit and the context and intent by which they commit these actions.

If you typically do good things, don't go around harming or hurting others, and focus on doing good deeds or even possess the capability of higher awareness or are aware of your thoughts and actions, then you might be categorized as a good person. Being a good person typically involves having the qualities that are known for making someone good such as humbleness, grace, lack of arrogance, love, kindness, joy and other traits that align with a beneficial state of mind and way of life.

Those who are moral people are usually people who abide by laws and rules that are either taught by society to be of benefit to others and to themselves, or those who follow the moral beliefs and laws of religious teachings and focus on those beliefs and live their ways mostly through these beliefs and ways of teachings. Good people don't generally go around doing negative or bad things or even harboring negative thoughts. They are constantly in a state of abundance and bliss, and they usually count their blessings and are in joy for the wonderful things and blessings they have been given and tend to count their blessings on a regular basis.

Now that doesn't mean that if you don't count your blessings all the time that you're not a good person. There are plenty of genuinely good people who also may not feel as if they are blessed with anything and might even complain in general or not be happy with their lives. That's completely ok, for that doesn't mean that people in this state of mind aren't good people either. It just means they haven't been able to focus on the positive, harbor it and appreciate all the goodness that is in their own life.

Good people possess the gift of being genuine and true good people. It's rare to find genuine people nowadays and it's harder to find people who are genuinely good people who don't harbor ill will towards others or possess the negative feelings of jealousy, hatred, greed, selfishness, and other dark attitudes that people can have. There are many negative people out there who tend to throw their negative and sickly attitudes towards others creating a downward spiral and disturbing a person's chi and creating chaos in the world and universe by spreading any form of negativity.

It's not always easy to determine if you're a good person. There are various factors that determine whether someone is considered to be a good person or not. The concept of good versus evil is a highly debated subject, and not can also be a very subjective topic to ponder upon. Do you do good deeds mostly? Do you harbor any evil or ill-will or intent within you? Do you enjoy doing good things over being an evil or malicious type of person?

The measurement of whether a person is good or not is very subjective to their character, their actions, their behaviors, their intent, their belief system, and their overall concept of awareness that they hold or levels of introspection. These factors can in fact determine whether a person is good or not overall.

A Person's Actions

Of course, there are people who seem like good people, but If they commit any major evils or acts of atrocity against another, then the concept of them being good people will tend to go out the window based on the actions they commit or what they have done and the level of evil their actions represent. A person's actions are key in determining whether a person is good or not. If a person does mostly good deeds, but some evil deeds that are considered to harm another person, then it's highly unlikely that they can be called or considered good people.

Luke might be a decent upstanding citizen on the surface. He does well at his job, gets along with his peers and co-workers, and is a highly talented worker. He treats his family with a lot of respect and seems to have no real issues when it comes to functioning in his daily life or with friends or family. However, Luke has a girlfriend named Mary, and Luke's behavior towards Mary is very different. He isn't very nice to Mary and is almost completely evil towards her and treats her with a huge lack of respect and is abusive to her most of the time. Luke has made Mary's life a living hell and takes all of his anger out on her most of the time and treats her and her children with a lot of disrespect and lack of care.

It's difficult to determine or claim that Luke could be construed as a good person in this case because of his actions towards Mary and her children. Abusive people tend to be extreme monsters towards their victims doing the most evil to them one can imagine, and very nice to others, where they play the Jekyll/Hyde persona, and treat their victims with hatred, disgust and can ruin lives and have a huge impact on a person's life. Luke would more than likely not be considered a good person because of the extreme level of evil behavior he displays today's his partner Mary, and because of the impact he has on her life.

A Person's Character:

A person's character is key in determining whether a person is a moral or good person or not. Generally, if a person abides by most moral standards or laws of society or religion, they can be considered a good person. Character is determined by a person's belief systems within, and how they present themselves to others and what they truly believe within themselves.

A person's character is their own personality, especially how reliable and honest someone might be. If someone is of good character, they are reliable and honest. If they are of bad character, they are considered unreliable and dishonest. The character of a person or place consists of all the qualities they have that make them distinct from other people or places.

If a person possesses bad or unfavorable characteristics such as being dishonest, rude, mean, abrasive, abusive, a bad person then they more than likely aren't going to be categorized as good people. If a person has good or moral upstanding characteristics such as those of honesty, goodness, decency, morality, positivity, helpfulness, then they are people who hold the character that can define them as good or decent people.

A Person's Behavior:

Actions are the deeds that are done, and behavior is the attitude someone conveys while doing it. For example, two people do the same job, which are hosting people at a store. Both do the same actions - greeters - but their behavior is vastly different, and it makes a huge difference with the way they impact and affect people who they interact with.

A person's behavior can have a huge impact in determining whether a person is considered a good or moral person or not. Behavior is basically the attitude and way in which a person acts. So, someone can commit specific actions, yet do them with poor or rude behavior and then it can have a different impact on the outcome or people will get a completely different attitude depending on the person's behavior. If a person commits actions and deeds with ill behavior, then they may be categorized as being mean, rude, abusive or anything negative or non-beneficial to a person or situation as opposed to being positive or good. Anything that which is positive is beneficial and anyone who commits behaviors with good intentions and with positive attitudes are doing something that is considered good, as opposed to doing them with ill behaviors or attitudes.

A Person's Intent:

A person's intent plays a key role as to whether they're good or decent people or not or what can categorize a person as good versus evil or not so good. Intent Is the reason for which a person does something and it's the deeper reasoning for which a person commits certain actions or deeds towards a stimulus, person, place or event. Intent is the motivation or purpose by which someone commits an action or deed. Intention is the idea or motive for which someone is going to do something.

If a person generally has good intent or good motives for which they are doing something you can say that they are doing something or they commit their actions with good intent, and that they are considered to be good people- this is in general of course, and if the intent by which they commit these actions is generally favorable all of this time. If their intentions by which they commit acts or actions towards others is negative, or they do things with ill intent, then they generally wouldn't be considered good people in general.

Intent is dependent upon the reasoning that a person commits the actions and deeds they do towards others. Most people in general aren't going to harbor ill-will or ill-intent towards others while committing basic daily actions, however some people may harbor bad intentions when it comes to the usual activities they do or what they are committing in daily life. Again, people may generally have good intent while doing things but may end up doing certain things with bad intentions. It all depends on the circumstances of course. If someone does major harm to a person with very bad intentions for no real reason, then they may not be considered to be good people even if the majority of the time they do good deeds or actions with good intent. That's because, major acts of evil or intentionally badly done acts can inflict severe harm on a person's life, psyche, and world and anything that is of negative benefit to a person or harmful is something that isn't allowed or something that is frowned upon when it comes to judging a person's morality, or determining the goodness a person possesses.

A Person's Belief System:

A person's belief system is religious and moral beliefs they hold as people and humans and the beliefs they were shaped with during their upbringing and their regular belief systems within their lives and how they generally live their life. A person's belief system has a huge role in shaping a person's moral levels, who they are and whether they are a good person or not. A person's belief system is extremely important, and it helps shape their personal beliefs when it comes to how they feel they should act in life, towards others and how they should generally treat others.

A belief system can consist of just basic general beliefs that a person holds, or a complex religious system that they are a part of such as Islam, Buddhism, Christianity etc. If a person follows a belief system that practices or teaches that we must be kind to others and do good deeds, and not harm others, and they live by this system, then they can generally be considered good people, as long as they practice this belief system regularly and fail to stray from it. If someone strays from a positive or beneficial belief system and practices negative, harmful, or evil actions regularly then it's hard to consider those people good people in general.

Most people aren't generally aware of the morals or beliefs they possess so practicing what a belief system teaches may not always be easy for them to do. It might seem tedious to them or even difficult.

People generally act the way they have from the beginning of time for them and tend to not stray from their general actions or behaviors. Most people don't usually possess a higher awareness or higher understanding of their actions or behaviors. It's important that people gain a higher awareness or knowledge of their actions in order to understand the concepts they do follow and believe in and in order to become better people in general.

A Person's Concept of Awareness

As stated earlier, most people don't generally possess the concept of higher awareness and most people aren't going to measure their daily actions or activities or even examine them wondering whether they follow a particular belief system, or whether their intent is pure with the actions they commit towards others. This is something that can be measured on a daily basis when it comes to anything a person does. A person should have complete and total awareness of anything they do in life, and understanding the reasoning by which they do these things in their own daily lives. Most people fail to possess this higher understanding, but for those who do and those who commit good deeds on purpose and with good intent, are considered to be good and decent, moral upstanding people on this planet.

Again, this is a rare concept to accept and to understand, for most people just don't possess this concept at all and are only focused on doing good, and with good intentions, and those who commit their actions with a higher awareness or understanding of them are considered to be good and upstanding people and their level of good can be measured in some form. People who do or commit actions with a general lack of awareness can still be considered good people, as long as their deeds and actions are of a beneficial nature, but they simply just lack the concept of awareness and understanding of the actions they are committing.

How to expand your moral awareness

The greatest way for a person to become a better person and grow into becoming more honest, decent people is by expanding their consciousness and by growing internally, which allows them to grow in morality. People need to have a constant understanding of the actions they commit, and the intent by which they commit the actions they do. People need to seek that which is of the higher good and focus on being better people than they were before and they can increase their moral awareness and their basic understanding of not only their own levels of morality, but the moral levels of their friends or family as well.

The way to expand your moral awareness is by shifting your awareness from one of lack of consciousness to one full of consciousness and awareness. It's by taking your subconscious mind and allowing it to act like your conscious mind, and letting your levels of awareness grow by examining every action you commit and knowing the exact intent by which you commit these very actions. Once you become aware of your actions and intent and do so knowingly, then you'll be able to harness your level of awareness and recognize your levels of morality and where you are as a person morally, though not everyone is going to have the same meter by which they are able to gauge their levels of morality and awareness.

A person will have to come to a full understanding of the concepts between right and wrong and what truly is considered moral or immoral and fully come to terms with knowing the levels of morality of every deed and action any person can commit and understand the levels of morality, good or bad each deed or action holds and the values of measurement they harbor as well. This takes time and practice to do, as a person will have to come to a greater understanding of the values of moral levels that come with each and every intent they hold and with each action that they undergo. Not everyone will have the wherewithal to possess this level of understanding or be able to fairly harness these specific judgments, so a person can really do the best they can when it comes to attempting to figure out how to measure the values of good versus bad when it comes to moral judgments, actions, and meters regarding this situation.

CHAPTER 5

MORALITY AND RELIGION

"Religion and morality are the essential pillars of civil society"
- George Washington

Goodness and religion go hand in hand, for most religions and religious beliefs and teachings revolve around specific laws set to govern civilized and once chaotic societies, and to protect society from being haphazard. It also paves the way for future societies and the ethics that these communities hold and protects society and the world in general from becoming victimized by a civilization that possesses a lack of morals.

Religion is the main teacher of morality. Without religion, society might end up being a chaotic mess of issues and problems, though there is always the justice system and the law which prevents evils and wrongdoings from taking place without punishment and putting that fear in people. However, religion is one of the main premises that teaches extreme amounts of morality to the world and to societies in order to prevent chaos and in order to ingrain these teachings into the very core, subconscious and souls of most human beings allowing them to be better and more moral people than they are without the values and teachings of religions. Now of course, there are many people who refuse to uphold these teachings, beliefs, or laws. They may even abide by them, but they lack the true concept of morality and spirituality.

How does religion play into the concept of morality?

Each and every religious book or teaching holds the key and the source to the truths about morality and the mysteries of the world and the universe. Every religious teaching and book has their own unique and rare belief system which allows great teachings and secrets to be told to those who access these beliefs and teachings, and they were all passed down from great scholars and teachers who had these words of wisdom to give to societies in order to do away with the unruliness and chaos that they were at the time.

Religion is the key to learning the truths about morality and though there are many out there who tend to criticize religion and call it a waste of time and a way to control society and people, it is in fact the complete opposite. Religion is a beautiful and special and important means of giving societies many important facts and a lot of information about the truths about the world and the planet, about life in general and has immensely important teachings regarding religion, love, life, morality, and spirituality.

Religions are often put down for being dogmatic and too centered on God. They are often criticized for being created by men who sought to control society and future societies. However, this is not the main reason that religion was created. Religion was created by God in order to teach humanity the truths about God and the truths about life, culture, people, our world, society and morality most importantly. God sent messengers or used messengers to speak to the people about the message He had to send out to humanity and to the world. Each and every religion has it's own special teaching, and also has its roots that all lead to the One and only God- who is the one who should be worshipped only and who we should learn these amazing special teachings and lessons from.

Religion is a wonderful belief system that allows us access to the hidden truths and beautiful messages that God Himself had to send out to humanity in general. Although Christianity has a strong base and belief in God, it does emphasize that there is a trinity and that there are three in one as God. Christianity still has many similar teachings to the other two monotheistic religions Islam and Judaism. Religion gives us the gift of being able to know what is or isn't allowed in society and life and gives us the very core teachings of God which are a beautiful special and wonderful example that anyone should be proud to learn about and to know. It allows people to be blessed with these wonderful teachings, which aren't just basic laws that govern society, and morals that we should live by, but also incorporate many varying spiritual aspects which make the teachings extremely deep and special and not just basic laws we need to live by in order to be good people on this planet or in order to live by the rules of God and of nature.

Without religion, society would be lost and would be unsure of what true morality or morals are, yet most people don't fully understand or grasp this concept. Most people in general simply do not understand the role that religion has played in shaping the morality of the world and of the planet. The Islamic teachings were sent to the Prophet Muhammed during a time of great chaos and paganism and actually eliminated the pagan beliefs that were present during the time he existed. Many religions and religious teachings were sent to various people or prophets in order to teach their societies and cultures about the existence of God, how to live in this world in a moral and decent manner, and to teach cultures and societies the truths about morality and ethics in their society and to create very important laws to live by as well.

Siddhartha Gautama was given very important life lessons as he slowly learned them through periods of what he considered enlightenment, nirvana, bliss and gaining of extreme awareness. The Buddha was given these great lessons to teach and to show to others the other hidden truths about life and reality. Each religion has a very important and specific set of teachings designed to teach and show humanity God's understanding and beliefs and the hidden secrets God is showing the world through these teachings and belief systems. The Buddhist teachings are about contentment and peace, and ways to end all suffering, and many definitions and meanings of the concept of suffering. Buddhism allows a person to gain a greater peace within themselves and teaches them many great concepts about how to live a person's life, through goodness, harmony, decency, the elimination of evil and of wrongdoing and to be a better person overall. Every religion helps and allows a person and society to shape their moral thinking and beliefs and are the great teachers of morality in all societies as long as humanity is of existence.

Islam as well is a religion that teaches greatly about peace and the end of evils or wrongdoing. Many religions hold a very common basic moral concept that there is a basic dislike for anything that might be harmful or actions that are harmful to others and a goodness for anything that is of benefit or good. All religions teach the basic moral laws and lessons which include how doing good or being a good person is a moral standard or basic, doing evil or flawed deeds is uncalled for or looked down upon or something that is completely forbidden and not allowed in society. Hurting others is taught against in almost all religions, as is any form of theft or taking of another person's life. These are incredibly important life lessons that every person must know, and to know that these lessons are coming from the source of the Creator is one amazing blessing and gift that we as humans are lucky or fortunate to possess or have been introduced to.

Religion is the basis for all moral teachings that civilized society today and rules and most laws abide by. Of course, most societies do have general and basic laws that constitute the justice and criminal system and allow for those who commit wrong or evil actions or illegal actions to be punished in some form. However, the concept of morality that religions teach is far more special and beautiful and gives humanity far greater spiritual and life lessons when it comes to learning about the truths with regards to ethics and life.

CHAPTER 6

WHAT IS AMORALITY?

Amorality is the concept of lacking morals in general and people who are amoral typically just lack the general concept of wanting to do what is right, just, moral or what might be good or beneficial to another person. Their main concern is what benefits them, and they behave through the lens of being very selfish, self-centered, driven people who care only about their own needs and desires. These are immoral people who lack most semblance of a conscience and only function based on what makes them happy with no regard to how it may hurt or affect another person. The concept of amorality or those who are amoral also know the difference between right and wrong but choose to do that which isn't right for different reasons.

The seven deadly sins were first enumerated in the sixth century by Pope Gregory I, and represent the many vices of immoral behavior. These are known as the cardinal sins or seven deadly vices, which are vanity, jealousy, anger, laziness, greed, gluttony, and lust. People who demonstrate these immoral behaviors are often said to be flawed in character and lack the basic mental knowing of the consequences of their actions. Most people who hold these traits simply don't care about what their actions do to others, and usually behave on a whim or even with ill-intent.

Amorality is the concept of being non-moral and a person that lacks morals feels as if their behaviors are ok in nature and has no regard to the actions they commit or the twisted intent by which they tend to commit many actions. Aristotle the great philosopher categorized amorality into two categories- wickedness and moral weakness.

Wickedness is deliberate or willful wrongdoing and, in most cases, the person tends to act as they want to act. The morally weak agent basically prefers not to act the way he does because he actually finds it to be wrong but ends up acting in this way regardless. He does so because of some form of influence or because of his own emotions. In the case of wickedness, the person has had some form of bad influence but acts on his own whims or lack of morals and feels no guilt or remorse in doing so.

Amorality is a huge problem and epidemic in society and always has and will be. This is because most humans are very flawed and do possess the semblance or notion of evil within themselves in some way, shape or form or in many ways. Most people lack the concept of higher awareness and goodness and lack empathy in general. This level of evil has grown as society has grown forth and as time has gone by, and you'll find the level of empathy and goodness has become less and less, while the concept of greed and selfishness has increased.

How to train the mind and soul

Upon training the mind and soul, you must first understand that the mind and soul were already trained and fully developed at and after birth and that any traumas associated after have helped pave the way for the development of the person that has formed as a result.

What is evil? Evil is the antithesis of good. It is the opposite of that which is beneficial, good, being of pleasant and good nature and anything that isn't associated with the concept of good. It is that of a harmful malicious intent and nature and there to do harm or hurt others and not do any form of good or help. That which is evil cannot have a place in an arena where good is present, for good always trumps evil whether you believe it or not.

Evil is the negativity that we face on a day-to-day basis, that which has consumed society and modern society and the preset of the world, the foundation for which the planet seems to revolve around in many cases and the negativity upon which many seem to flourish unjustifiably. With evil comes no real flourishing, only that which is negative, harmful and non-beneficial for others and for the planet itself. It is important to be against that which is evil or that which represents any form of evil.

Evil is that which is frowned upon in the moral world for evil is about doing deeds and actions that are harmful or that which lacks benefit and can hurt others in a major way. Evil deeds and actions are generally not ok to commit and evil is that which is easily disliked upon but that which many people seem to commit for their own personal reasons.

Evil is commonly referred to the act or actions that go directly against what is to be considered good. Good, or a set or morals and beliefs, have differed between the many generations that have existed over time. Evil is commonly referred to immorally bad behavior and some that causes pain and suffering towards others and can create havoc and negatives in and upon the world and in society in general.

Evil is more than often used to talk about profound wickedness, and immorality in general and anything that is against good and is of harmful or non-beneficial in nature. In certain religious contexts, evil can be defined as a supernatural force, though evil generally can define any action, deed, intent, thought, or belief, that a person can take upon towards another and in a negative manner. Evil is nothing to be taken lightly for the concept of evil actions have a long-lasting and profound negative on the planet and world and society as a whole.

Evil is the concept of causing unnecessary suffering and pain and of not being of benefit but doing the opposite of that which is good and beneficial. The modern English word evil, and its similars such as the German "Ubel" and Dutch Euvel, are considered to come from a proto-Germanic reconstructed form of ubilaz comparable to the Hittite "Huwapp." Other later Germanic forms include "evel, ifel, ufel, evel, and Old Saxon Ubil.

The root meaning of the word evil is similar to modern German Ubel, with the basis of of social or religious transgression.

Evil and religion:

Most religions seek to teach the wrongness of evil and how evil is something that causes chaos and disorder and that needs to be eliminated or lessened. Most religions tend to preach that wrongdoing is looked down upon and that we should spread goodness, love, and peace over doing that which is wrong, frowned upon or evil in nature. In some forms of thought, evil is also sometimes perceived as the dualistic antagonistic binary opposite to good, where good should prevail and evil should be defeated. There are many thought-forms and cultures that preach this principle of defeating evil in some form, as opposed to committing evil actions or cultivating it. In turn, good is what should be cultivated or taught and practiced in greater forms, and evil should be done away with.

In cultures with Buddhist spiritual influence, both good and evil are perceived as part of an antagonistic duality that itself must be overcome through achieving Nirvana. The ethical questions regarding good and evil are subsumed into three major areas of study: meta-ethics concerning the nature of good and evil, normative ethics, concerning how we ought to behave, and applied ethics, concerning particular moral issues.

Islamic belief regarding sin

Islamic beliefs concerning evil date back to 600 AD where the Prophet Muhammad taught staunchly against evil and its principles and taught his followers to practice and preach that which is good and beneficial to others only. Within Islam, it is considered essential to believe that all comes from God, whether it is perceived as good or bad by individuals; and things that are perceived as *evil* or *bad* are either natural events (natural disasters or illnesses) or caused by humanity's free will. Much more the behavior of beings with free will, then they disobey God's orders, harming others or putting themselves over God or others, is considered to be evil.

Evil in Islam is absolute and anyone who practices any form of evil is disobeying God directly. Islam teaches against anything that harms others and has very staunch teachings against abuse or any kind of evil, harmful act or deed or any kind of wrongdoing of any given nature. The teachings of Islam go against any kind of evil or harm to exist. The teachings of Islam the hadith teach that "whoever of you sees wrong being committed, let him change it with his hand (i.e. by force). If he is unable to do that, then with his tongue, and if he is unable to do that, then with his heart."

Islam has teachings regarding the origins of evil. The Qur'an teaches that evil originates from the refusal of Satan/the Devil to bow down to Adam when ordered to by God. For his disobedience, Satan was cast out of Heaven by Allah.

Muslim teachings believe that individuals should know, which actions are evil and will contribute to the suffering of others, and which actions are good. This inner sense of right and wrong is called *fitrah*. Muslims believe all human beings are born with this sense or instinct to live according to the teachings and laws of God.

Islam teaches that suffering can be caused by the selfishness and evil of human beings. This selfishness and evil leads to bad decisions. By following God's path, Muslims can overcome suffering in their own lives and help to ease the suffering of others. This is a specific path that is described in the Holy teachings of Islam.

Muslims believe in following the teachings of God and to follow all of his commandments. Muslims are also expected to follow Allah's example of justice, mercy and forgiveness in their treatment of other people. When a Muslim witnesses someone who is suffering, they should treat them with mercy and compassion, the same way God would, and if they witness an evil action, they should respond with acts of justice or kindness and a way of dealing with the evil action.

Christian belief regarding sin

Christianity teaches that evil and suffering in this life is a preparation for Heaven. A place, or a state of mind, associated with God and the afterlife. Evil and suffering give people a chance to become better people and improve their souls. Christianity teaches that God will reward them in Heaven.

God has given people free will. He has shown people how they should obey the *Ten Commandments* and follow Jesus' life and teaching. It is then up to human beings to decide if they want to follow God's rules and laws.

God has a plan for people's lives that they may not always understand. This may include evil and suffering, but Christians should trust and have faith in God's plan. Evil from a Christian point of view is a result of a world that was corrupted. According to the Christian point of view in Genesis, there was no evil after the creation of man. Evil came about after humans became corrupted and went down the wrong path taken.

After the Garden of Eden and the fall of Adam and Eve, Cain and Abel, and the murder of Abel paved the way for bloodshed and violence in the world today. Greed, hate, jealousy, pride, and wickedness became part of the human psychology and these vices have continued to contribute to a large extent, the evil we see in the world today. The Christian worldview teaches that we are all descendants of Adam and Eve and that we are similar to our ancestors and have inherited this form of sin from them.

Buddhist teachings regarding evil

The Buddhist attitude towards evil is not to deny its existence nor to reconcile its presence in the world, but to observe carefully, and study its nature and causes in order to eliminate it. In the Dhammapada, the Buddha dictates: "Never commit any evils; but practice all the goods."

Evil is a characteristic that is specific to some groups or to some people. Evil can also be portrayed as an external force similar to Satan or some kind of creation that causes people to do different kinds of evil. Buddhism teaches us that evil is something we create, not something we are or some outside force that might be a part of us.

Buddhism doesn't typically believe in the concept of good versus evil- it looks at everything in a dualistic manner. Evil as a characteristic is contrary to Buddhism.

Many religions have varying teachings when it comes to their belief system regarding evil and morality. While most religions do teach against doing anything harmful, there are specific religions such as Islam and Christianity, Judaism and any monotheistic religion that teaches against any form of evil or wrongdoing. There are also religions that have varying or other perspectives on the teachings of right versus wrong, and good versus evil. These religions include Hinduism and Buddhism and they both have unique views on the concept of religion and evil.

Chapter 7

Morality And Ethics In Society Today

Through the idea of the supreme good as object and final end of the pure practical reason the moral law leads to religion, that is, to the recognition of all duties as divine commands, not as sanctions, that is, as arbitrary commands of an alien will which are contingent in themselves, but as essential laws of every free will in itself, which, however, must be looked on as commands of the supreme Being, because it is only from a morally perfect (holy and good) and at the same time all-powerful will, and consequently only through harmony with this will, that we can hope to attain the highest good, which the moral law makes it our duty to take as the object of our endeavour."
—Immanuel Kant

How Do Morals Affect Regular Society?

Morals play a huge role in shaping society. They provide a guideline for individuals to make ethical decisions, guide behavior and establish societal norms and values. They contribute to social fun, and the overall ethics and play a huge role of values in a society.

Society is shaped by the morals and ethics we believe in as a whole. In some cultures, certain ethics and principles are valued differently than they are in other cultures, so the belief system and way of life varies greatly. For example, in some cultures, personal autonomy is highly valued which leads to a focus on personal rights and personal freedoms. Other cultures, namely collectivist cultures, prioritize the well-being of the group and emphasize communal harmony, which can influence moral behaviors and the way a culture thinks about the particular given situation. Other cultural values can shape moral differences and beliefs as a whole.

Without morals, society would be a basket case and at a huge loss. The world would lack basic civility, there would be no judgment for crime or punishment, and there would be chaos everywhere on the planet. Morals ensure that there is a righteous and just punishment for every ill or evil action out there and that there is an equal reaction for the evils that are being done out there towards people and actions in society.

Can you have morals without religion?

The answer is yes- you can definitely have morals without religion. That is because religion is a set of beliefs that contain teachings regarding morality, but religion is not the ultimate source of morality or morality itself. So, you can definitely have morals without the concept of religion of course, but many of the morals you might believe in or partake in are actually presented in religion and the beliefs are a part of religion and what is taught to others through religious teachings. Morals are a set of standards of ethics or ethical beliefs with regards to what is good or regarded as not right in this world. So you can definitely have morals without religion or religious beliefs present but the morals you do hold are going to also be a part of religious beliefs as well more than likely.

Do animals have morals?

Animals do have and possess the culpability or sense of knowing the difference between right and wrong and do have some subset of morals. Animals also possess a higher consciousness, but they lack the ability to relay their abilities or set of beliefs, or ways of thinking as effectively as humans can. Animals have the ability to speak and talk through their tones and voices, but they aren't able to communicate using English, though that doesn't mean that they don't possess the capability of higher or other ways of thinking. In fact, animals are a lot like humans in the way they think, behave, react, and act towards stimuli and scenarios and situations in life. How does one know that animals possess these capabilities.

Well, if a person is around animals, or has one as a companion, roommate, child, or pet then they will soon learn that animals can and do communicate not only with each other but very effectively with humans as well, and it's discoverable that animals do hold the capability of having and feelings ideations of something that is good or bad or evil or not evil. They know the difference between right and wrong in many cases yet sometimes don't hold the higher knowledge of these basic morals. That is because animals are a part of nature too, are mammalian in nature, and live by their own moral code. They also hold the same sets of beliefs humans do which involves not doing any kind of wrongdoing or harm, doing good unto others, and being generally good peaceful creatures just like many humans may feel.

There are many studies that have been done throughout varying animals special and more than 90 percent have shown that animal's behavior is actually positive or what they call prosocial. So overall, animals have a great sense of morality because they live by their own set of moral codes that are innate and that which nature created. Animals are generally very positive, beautiful special deep-thinking, intuitive, peace-loving creatures who enjoy love, goodness and positivity and they really don't react well to negativity the way many humans are, though there are many negative humans who tend to thrive on being negative. You don't find much negativity, evil and hatred among animals so there are people who tend to feel as if animals are in fact more moral than humans.

Do Humans possess basic ethics?

In general, most humans do seem to hold the basic ethics of living decent lives for themselves, their families, and their loved ones. If people weren't good in general, then the world would be a very chaotic place, and though it does seem to be chaotic, it would be far worse if people possessed a lot of evil and committed acts of evil all the time, rather than living decent honest lives. However, deep within themselves, many humans do hold the notion of harboring various forms of darkness and as a result, there might be areas in their life where they display this darkness or evil, whether it's amongst friends, family, loved ones, in a relationship, towards their children etc. So overall, humans do hold basic ethics otherwise the world would be a very difficult place to live in, if people didn't live by the golden rule in some form, or harbor some form of decency, goodness, or ethics.

What is the concept of having a conscience?

This is Conscience, and, from the nature of the case, its very existence carries on our minds to a Being exterior to ourselves; or else, whence did it come?" —John Henry Newman, "

The concept of having a conscience is the idea of a person, having a means by which they have specific standards within their mind, such as the basis of right versus wrong, and by which they usually partake in doing what is right or that which is good or beneficial for the whole or greater good. You can commit evil acts or deeds using your conscience, but the basic lessons are to teach us that we should commit just and decent acts with the virtuous or moral portion of our mind or brain, rather than something that is negative or harmful.

A conscience is the inherent ability of every healthy human being to perceive what is right and what is wrong and, on the strength of this perception, to be able to know what to do, which is right or correct, rather than what is wrong. More than just 'gut instinct', our conscience is a 'moral muscle'. By informing us of our values and principles, it becomes the standard we use to judge whether or not our actions are ethical.

Jennifer just had a test in her class, and she ended up cheating on her test. Jennifer knows that what she did was incorrect, and her conscience ended up telling her it just wasn't right, so in turn she ended up having a guilty conscience for doing this very act or deed. She knew that her act was immoral, and her belief or idea in what she committed was the very act of possessing a conscience, yet in this case it was a negative act that was done.

Many various great thinkers and philosophers had different theories regarding consciousness and how they felt it interplayed with the way a person felt and thought and how it affected morality and life. Socrates expresses real existence as the universal 'I,' as the consciousness which rests in itself; but that is the good as such, which is free from existent reality, free from individual sensuous consciousness of feeling and desire, free from the theoretically speculative thought about nature, which, if indeed thought, has still the form of being and in which I am not certain of my existence.

This freedom which is contained therein, the fact that consciousness is clearly present in all that it thinks, and must necessarily be at home with itself, is in our time constantly and plainly demanded; the substantial, although eternal and in and for itself, must as truly be produced through me; but this my part in it is only the formal activity. Thus Socrates' principle is that man has to find from himself both the end of his actions and the end of the world, and must attain to truth through himself.

The medieval philosopher Thomas Aquinas believed our conscience emerged from *synderesis:* the 'spark of conscience'. He explained that conscience proceeds from a habitual disposition that qualifies the human intellect. He literally meant the human mind's ability to understand the world in moral terms. Conscience was the process by which a person brought the principles of *synderesis* into a practical situation through our decisions.

For Immanuel Kant, conscience, is a built-in element of his practical reasoning, whereas for Aristotle there is the awareness resulting from the apparentness of one's end and the means best corresponding to it, this awareness being an imagination and sensitivity which develops in itself.

Kant sees morality as the endeavor to find the principles and categories of knowledge which explain our understanding in action. The central issue in his moral philosophy is therefore what one should be doing. Practical reason is therefore reason as Kant means it in general but is used in a particular way. Kant sees practical reason as creating its own object.

John Henry Newman had a different view on conscience. Newman does an assessment of the unity of his consciousness and his existence, which proves that his consciousness is proof of his existence, since one can't be aware of the latter without being aware of the former. He further shows that he has an immediate awareness of his consciousness and doesn't have to figure it out or believe in it since there is enough proof it exists.

> *"This is Conscience, and, from the nature of the case, its very existence carries on our minds to a Being exterior to ourselves; or else, whence did it come?" —John Henry Newman*

John Henry Newman observes that conscience commands him, and that this command includes "praise, blame, promise, a future, and the unseen. Newman further shows that there is a *personal* dimension intrinsic to these special qualities of the feelings of conscience.

He focuses on these special feelings to show their *interpersonal* nature of them, revealing that these feelings could not be experienced were it not through a relationship with another person:

> *"The feeling is one analogous or similar to that which we feel in human matters towards a* person *whom we have offended; there is a tenderness almost tearful on going wrong, and a grateful cheerfulness when we go right, which is just what we feel in pleasing or displeasing a father or revered superior." —John Henry Newman, "Proof of Theism,"*

Newman shows this personal dimension is not completely similar to those experienced by human beings.

Newman demonstrates that the personal dimension is not completely similar to those experienced with human beings but has a divine dimension that is similar in its supreme authority- like an unseen father. Both Kant and Newman's theories attempt to prove the transcendental nature of our higher conscience. This is the very fact that God and the divine are present within our conscience, and that for this very reason we have a soul.

CHAPTER 8

THE LAWS OF NATURE

The laws of nature can be defined as natural laws that govern life, society and morality and by which nature occurs in this world and how the inhabitants of this planet are governed and ruled by. There are many varying laws and contexts that can be defined and described in this section, for you can find a host of different laws that can describe natural causes and actions and ways nature can be ruled and governed including both humans and animals.

The structures and phenomena encountered in the real world can be described in terms of the laws of nature in the form of principles which are universally valid. The laws of nature describe those phenomena, events and results which occur in the interplay between matter and energy. Statements about natural events can be classified according to the degree of certainty, namely: models, theories, hypotheses, paradigms, speculations, and fiction.

The theory of natural law claims that humans possess an intrinsic sense of right and wrong that governs our reasoning and behavior. The concepts of natural law stem from the times of Plato and Aristotle and were practiced by great thinkers such as Mahatma Gandhi and Martin Luther King Jr. Natural law is constant throughout time and across the globe because it is based on human nature, not on culture or customs. Natural law is opposed to theories that laws are socially constructed and created by people. Natural laws exist in many fields out there from philosophy to economics.

The laws of nature and the theory of natural law states that human beings possess intrinsic values that govern our reasoning and behavior. It states that there are universal moral standards that are seen across time periods and societies because these standards form the basis of a just society.

The laws of nature are the laws of ethics that hold true to their intrinsic values and beliefs. These are the laws and rules that we as a society need to live and abide by in order to grow as a whole, be ruled by justly, and be sustained as a civilized society through.

There are several natural laws that can come into effect that have a huge impact on the human population and how actions on this plane of existence are governed and measured. There are certain fundamentals that give us insight and direction into how everything works including how to be better people and receive better results as people and even as leaders in our lives. These fundamentals are called the Seven Natural Laws through which everyone and everything is governed. They are the laws of : Attraction, Polarity, Rhythm, Relativity, Cause and Effect, Gender/Gestation and Perpetual Transmutation of Energy. There is no priority or order or proper sequence to these particular rules. They also may apply randomly since they are part of the natural laws you'll find within the metaphysical method of thinking.

The Law of Attraction:

The law of attraction is a very popular and well-known rule and law that can govern our universe and that is established as a factor in assisting people in reaching their goals and achievements in life. A vibration is a form of energy that is either positive or negative. Whatever is like tends to attract something that is of a similar nature, and that is the basis for the law of attraction.

This particular thoughtform teaches that a person attracts people, resources, and ideas that are in alignment with their dominant thoughts. Thoughts and feelings are energy. Whenever you are sensitive to someone else's feelings, when you are aware of your own feelings, this is a conscious perception of a vibration.

A vibration is a particular energy that is positive or negative. You have the power to choose your thoughts or change them by what you choose to think about, by how you speak to yourself and others. Listen to your thoughts and ask yourself if they are congruent with the person you are or want to be. The energy you project is what you will receive based on the thoughtforms that you are sending out and what you are intending.

With this belief system, you really have to focus on what you want and on the task at hand, and it's important that you eliminate the negative thoughts and ways of thinking. This is a process and something that takes time and practice.

The Law of Polarity

Everything in the Universe has an equal or an exact opposite. Teach yourself to pause and reflect on all sides. Think of two points of view and how they need each other. Within all change, (which is constant), there are actually two points of view that are in tension yet need each other - these are known as Polarities. You cannot have one without the other so, to some degree, you must embrace the opposite to find a way to move forward. Resistance comes from those with the opposing yet equally important point of view.

They may prefer stability over change, which shows up as holding onto the best of the past and the fear of losing it through change. In general, we accept that there is good and bad, positive, and negative and everything that comes with it. Everything has an opposite. Joy and sorrow are both beautiful; you cannot have one without the existence of the other. You cannot have one facet of a dynamic without having the other as a part of it in some form.

The Law Of Relativity

The law of relativity simply states that anything that happens is basically relative. You can't define something without having something to compare it to. For some making millions of dollars is a big deal, while for others it almost seems like not a lot of money. Everything we do and compare to on this planet is relative. This law states that the mind is always comparing any given something in order to position the situation that's given at hand.

You will need to be relative to what is and focus your goals on whatever you want or need for the right reasons. Focus on what you want and need and everything will fall into place without having to compare one thing to another.

The Law of Cause and Effect

Everything we do on this plane of existence has a cause and effect, like a ripple that comes shining through affecting everything in its path. Your actions impact everything and everyone around you and that energy goes on to impact others beyond that. If you send good thoughts and positive energy out you will receive the same or similar back, and of course the opposite is also true. We are the great creators of what we want to happen on this planet and just knowing this is a very powerful thought to live by and commit to.

When you take "responsibility" for being the cause of everything in your life, you empower yourself in many grand ways. It's important to understand that anything we do has an effect on ourselves, and on others as well and that we must choose our actions, behaviors and words wisely before acting upon them.

The Law of Rhythm

The law of rhythm states that everything that happens in the universe does so through a rhythmic flow, sort of like a pendulum, and everything in existence is involved in a dance flowing and swinging back and forth. There is always an action and a reaction; an advance and a retreat, a rising and a lowering. The seasons of the year have a rhythm to them, as do how we eat, sleep, and wake up. To be a successful musician, you have to be in rhythm with the music and with musical tones as well.

Rhythm works everywhere. In life and anything you're working on. You're in rhythm when you're not rushing or doubting; you're playing the music and in great sync and harmony and you're not rushing or trying to get through things- you're doing everything the way it was supposed to be done.

The Law of Gestation

Gestation is the period of time it takes for something to come into form. A baby goes through a gestation period of nine months. There are many other gestation periods that exist throughout a person's life that come into play within this type of scenario.

This is the creative law. This law decrees that all seeds most importantly "thought seeds" have a gestation period before they manifest. It takes an appropriate amount of time for a thought, image, or creation to move into its physical counterpart. You might create a plan of action, and then look for the appropriate time to introduce it to the people who are involved.

The Law of Transmutation of Energy

Energy is flowing into our consciousness constantly, and we transform this energy into whatever we choose through our focus of attention at the time. This formless energy is there to be shaped by our minds. Energy isn't ever created or destroyed. It simply moves from one form into another.

The good thing is that our thoughts have the ability to transmute from the non-physical to physical all the time. You can use this energy to create leadership, goals and drive for yourself and use it to challenge others and to bring power and creativity into your life and in whatever it is that you partake in.

There are various arguments concerning the laws of nature and specific elements that are known to validate the laws and are conditions necessary for them being an element of a law of nature. These are that they are factual truths, not logical ones, that they are true for every time and every place in the universe, that they contain no proper names, are universal or statistical claims, and that they are conditional claims and not categorical ones.

Numbers and scientific terms can represent factual truths, and "every number has a double" can explain a logical truth. There are no laws of nature that hold just for the planet earth, nor are there laws that are set only for specific time periods or eras- they must be factual and true for every time and place in the universe. Laws of nature must not contain any proper names but can only have specific and distinct descriptions. All copper conducts electricity is a law of nature and contains specific information and can be considered a statistical claim and therefore can be categorized in this manner. They also must be conditional claims and not categorical ones.

The laws of nature can be defined as natural laws that govern and assist with defining the universe and are the means by which the necessity of morality is upheld within society. There are several universal laws of nature that allow a person to uphold moral ideations, standards and beliefs. These laws further define the standards by which the justice system is developed. Many of these laws are also recognized within the religious belief structures and texts that are taught to humanity in order to further allow us to be educated and understand what the true laws of nature are structured to be and what they represent.

Natural law is a theory in ethics and philosophy that says that human beings possess intrinsic values that govern their reasoning and behavior. Natural law maintains that these rules of right and wrong are inherent in people and are not created by society or court judges. Animals too, follow these laws and these are the ways that nature intended things to be. Disorder, chaos and disarray are not the way nature meant for people to live. It did intend for people to live in a state of harmony, peace and joy.

You should not harm, hurt, or kill any individual

Theft or any form of taking that which isn't yours is unallowed

Committing any egregious sin against another isn't allowed in society

Having issues or rifts with your neighbors or friends or hurting them isn't allowed

Cheating on your spouse isn't allowed in society and should be looked down upon

It is of great importance that a person understands that the ten commandments brought forth by Moses had a huge bearing in creating the laws and rules that we encounter today and in shaping the way people think when it comes to morality and within society. Religious dogma, texts and teachings all held great bearings when it came to determining moral codes in society and in today's world and planet that we reside in. Religious texts and beliefs hold many of these specific teachings in order to shape and mold societal beliefs and these are also laws that uphold the justice and criminal systems in all societies.

It is important that a person not harm or kill or have any contact with the harm of any individual basically. Harming an individual is a grave sin and is something that is a universal law of nature when it comes to the rules in society pertaining to the treatment of others.

Hurting or taking the life of another is a completely forbidden act and is a universally known law that is undertaken by society as a whole concerning other people and the treatment of humanity as a whole.

Theft or any form of stealing of another's personal property or material items is not allowed within the universal laws of nature and within the context of the criminal and justice system and the rules it upholds. Both the Natural Law Theory and the Kantian Ethical Theory agree that theft is unethical behavior. According to the Natural Law Theory, theft is a morally repugnant act because it infringes on the rights of other people, upsets the natural order, and does not work toward the advancement of the common good.

Committing any kind of sin against another is frowned upon such as lying, cheating or backbiting or talking bad about another. These basic negative behaviors are looked down upon or discouraged in a general consensus and there are repercussions in general for committing these very actions. They cause disharmony and disruption in society in general and cause great issues and harm amongst people and in various situations. These kinds of sins can cause issues in a person's life and can cause many major issues in society as a whole. Family, loved ones, friends, and whole communities can be affected by these negative actions.

Love thy neighbor is a major commandment and something that is taught by religious texts and books, and is an important element in following the natural laws of the universe. You will want to be nice to your friends and neighbors and be in good standing with them and not create chaos or havoc amongst those who are living in close proximity to you or with those who are close to you in any form. It's important to be in good standing with those close to you and not to commit or do any actions that might be of harm to them in any way in order to follow the natural laws of the universe, world, and society.

Cheating on one's partner is another grave sin that should be and is looked down upon. Hester Prynne of The Scarlet Letter was branded an outcast for committing adultery and branded with the letter A, and in general, the concept of cheating and adultery is still looked down upon in society today. If someone cheats on their partner or spouse, there are severe consequences that occur with these actions including the wrecking of the person's house and their family life, sexually transmitted diseases, marital issues and rifts, and the overall disarray and disharmony of the actions being committed.

In many religious societies, adultery is looked down upon and even punished today. Although adultery shouldn't have formal or any form of capital punishment involved, it is something that is morally and ethically wrong and should be done away with or looked down upon or punished in one form or another. Adultery is one sin or misconduct that isn't accepted by most in any civilized society and will always be unaccepted. Adultery will always be looked down upon by natural laws of ethics and will always be something that will be perceived as wrong or an ill action or deed.

Natural law is an ethical theory that claims that humans are born with a certain moral compass that guides behaviors. These inherited rules essentially distinguish the "rights" and "wrongs" in life. Under natural law, everyone is afforded the same rights, such as the right to live and the right to happiness. Natural law shapes many of our laws, business policies, and human rights agendas. However, unlike these systems, its rules do not change and really tend to represent everyone.

Natural laws help humans guide societies towards living in ways that are righteous or just and allow societies as a whole to live upstanding lives, rather than lives of disarray, chaos, lack of justice, and lack of government. It is understood that we must not hurt each other, steal another's life, take another's property, along with many other natural laws that are present in life and society. However, it is important that we live by these rules and laws and not just understand their meaning and existence and allow them to guide our lives and let us be a better more ethical and moral planet overall.

CHAPTER 9

MORALITY AND JUSTICE

What is the concept of justice and how does it apply to the sense of morality? The concept of justice is very important when it comes to rationalizing and understanding the semblance of morality. Justice is about attaining a balance of what is good and right on this planet and morality is about the morals and ethics we harness in general with regards to being good and upstanding people. It is of extreme importance that we strive to be the best people we can be and that our concept of morality and justice is one of the utmost importance and of good in general. Our morals reflect who we are as people and the actions we undergo and partake in are symbolic of the kind of people we are.

Justice is an important part of morality for justice is about upholding a system of laws and rules and doing what is morally right or superior when it comes to a specific set of things done or criteria. Justice is regarded as the greatest and most fundamental moral virtue, taking precedence over all others. Equally, however, justice remains the most contentious moral, ethical, political, and social issue of our time.

Justice is one of the most important moral values in the spheres of law and politics. Legal and political systems that maintain law and order are desirable, but they cannot accomplish either unless they also achieve justice. Justice is also fairness, and with fairness comes a subset of moral standards by which this fairness is determined. Without the idea of morality, there would be no concept of justice.

The most fundamental principle of justice-one that has been widely accepted since it was first defined by Aristotle more than two thousand years ago-is the principle that "equals should be treated equally and unequals unequally." This principle is often expressed in this form: "Individuals should be treated the same, unless they differ in ways that are relevant to the situation in which they are involved."

Justice is an extremely important part of the concept of ethics, and when evaluating any moral decision, we need to come to terms with whether a person is being treated fairly or not. The justice system heavily relies on the concept of fairness and ethical standards by which laws and rules are created and governed by. Without the concept of morality, the justice system might not be what it is today, for most laws and rules of a justice system are based upon moral standards and ethical notions and the concept of doing what is right or good when it comes to deciding what is or isn't fair. There are various kinds of justice, and ways of describing them.

The great thinkers and philosophers had many varying opinions on the concept of justice and this ideation was written about in many philosophical texts throughout history. Plato and Aristotle defined justice as a component of general virtue, that is the excellence of a thing, or something possessed by a thing or some quality of a thing that enables the thing to do what it does very well.

Plato's view on justice

In the renowned Republic, Plato defines justice as a critical virtue necessary to establish societal order. At a personal level justice embodies personal order, that is individual goodness and obedience of laws. Plato felt justice was an order and duty of the parts of the soul, and justice is to the soul as health is to the body. He felt justice was a harmonious strength, and the effective harmony of the whole. Plato believed justice was the true principle of social life.

At a societal level justice is synonymous with piety, which symbolizes a relationship with the gods and the laws governing the

Republic or State. According to Plato, justice in life is that different parts of the soul are placed in their proper place, and in social life, each individual and each class is placed the same way. Plato believed that human nature is made from, wisdom, courage, and appetite. Plato's justice does not state a conception of rights but of duties and is similar to true liberty. Justice is a quality of moral life according to Plato.

To Plato, justice demands division of society into three classes representing the elements of reason, spirit and appetite, one man, and one work. Plato's belief is that justice is the fundamental virtue, the greatest of the virtues belonging to each of the three souls. He felt that man must be educated in order to reach justice and through it to become like God.

Aristotle's view on justice

Aristotle's concept of justice was concerned with what is lawful and fair, hence the coining of the special forms of justice, distributive and retributive Justice. Retributive Justice is concerned with repairing the wrongs or crimes committed, thereby ensuring that when societal rules have been violated, wrongs are righted through some legitimate mechanism. Distributive Justice means that to every man would be accorded dues, rights, and rewards according to merit, effort or contribution.

Aristotle, a disciple of Plato, believed that justice is the very essence of the state, and that no government can endure for a long time unless it is founded on a correct mode of justice. It is with this consideration in view that Aristotle proceeds to set forth his theory of justice.

According to Aristotle, justice in an individual is the harmony in the human soul, and in society is equality and proportion in the concept of values. In Aristotle's political philosophy, essential criterion of justice is treating equals equally and un-equals unequally but in proportion to their differences.

Augustine's view on justice

Augustine's philosophical views on justice represent a tension between his Christian beliefs and life under Roman rule. In his work, The City of God, Augustine states that all humans are children of God, and are therefore equal and worthy of similar treatment by man and State. He also noticed that the Romans were self-servicing and used force and injustice rather than right in their everyday dealings. This led to his conclusion that the Roman Empire was unjust because it steered from the pursuit of love, peace, and commitment to service. Other Greek philosophers felt similarly about the injustice of the Roman Empire with regards to fairness, and the rules and laws regarding it.

According to Augustine, Rome was unjust, and its rules and laws could not be upheld or really weren't. He felt it was moral to revolt against such an unjust system, since there was no obligation to obey these laws. Another philosopher, Aquinas felt that justice was an extension of natural law, which is God's law. Therefore, he felt that a person is in harmony with and should constantly act according to the natural law. These philosophers defined justice as stemming from Christian morality and roots and the belief in God, and felt it was God's purpose and wish for humankind.

Kant's view on justice

Immanuel Kant's philosophy is an example of deontology, which is the science of duty, and is duty-based morality. He felt that what is right or just is inherently right, independent of its consequences or outcomes. This absolute or categorical necessity requires a just system or person to respect the rights of others regardless of associated circumstances or consequences. According to Kant's theory, Categorical Imperative, Justice should be unconditional. Kant feels categorial imperatives are commands or moral laws all people should follow, regardless of situation, and these are important for everyone.

Kant's categorial imperative idea of justice and life is such that it is our duty to act in such a manner that we would want everyone else to act in a similar manner in circumstances towards all other people. Kant expressed this as the Categorical Imperative. Act according to the means or way that you would desire all other people to follow, as if it were a universal law.

Kant grounds Justice in freedom or autonomy of moral agents, and the need to respect others to live their lives as they wish. Kant believed strongly in morals, and also felt it was necessary to restrict freedom in accordance with universal law. This is a form of retributive justice which is a type of intervention that seeks to restrict specific kinds of behaviors from becoming universal.

The laws of justice are there to ensure that every member of society receives fair and equal treatment. Just establishments will create rules that instill fairness and equal treatment which in turn creates happier and more satisfied people, whereas institutions which harbor injustice will cause upheavals or rebellion amongst the people for which it supports.

Distributive Justice

Distributive justice refers to the extent to which society's institutions ensure that benefits and burdens are distributed among society's members in ways that are fair and just. This type of justice is called economic justice as well, and it is concerned with giving society members all that is fair or justice. When the institutions of a society distribute benefits or burdens in unjust ways, there is a strong presumption that those institutions should be changed. As an example, several slavery institutions in the pre-civil war were condemned as unjust because they treated people differently based on their race.

Retributive Justice

A second important kind of justice is retributive or corrective justice. Retributive justice refers to the extent to which punishments are fair and just. In general, punishments are held to be just to the extent that they take into account relevant criteria such as the seriousness of the crime and the intent of the criminal and will discount other criteria that is not relevant such as race or gender.

This type of justice is based on the idea that people deserve to be treated in the same way they treat others. It is an approach that justifies punishment as a response to past injustice or wrongdoing. The main idea is that the offender has gained unfair advantage through his or her behavior, and that punishment will set the person's behavior straight. Basically, those who do not follow the basic rules should be brought to justice and should be penalized for their transgressions.

Compensatory Justice

Another important kind of justice is compensatory justice. Compensatory justice refers to the extent to which people are fairly compensated for their injuries by those who have injured them. Just compensation is proportional to the loss inflicted on a person. This is the kind of justice that is at stake in debates over damage to workers' health in coal mines. Some feel that mine owners should compensate the workers whose health has been ruined.

Procedural Justice

Procedural justice emphasizes that a fair and unbiased procedure must be followed when serving justice to perpetrators. Procedural justice is there to ensure that all members of society feel as if everyone gets a fair trial, and that their wrongdoings are proven in an unbiased court or peers. This type of justice is thought of in terms of 'innocent until proven guilty,' in a court system of a functioning democratic system with a judiciary.

Corrective Justice

Corrective justice is a principle of fairness that deals with the rectifying of wrongs done to individuals. A wrong is known to be an action that causes harm or infringes upon the rights of others. Corrective justice says that the wrongdoer must make right the harm that it has done to another person. This can be done as compensation to the individual or some form of restitution.

One example of corrective justice are legal disputes between parties and private lawsuits that take place where one person seeks compensatory damage from another. The concept regarding this kind of justice is to restore moral balance and make things right by undoing the harm or wrong that was done, along with any monetary or other type of compensation.

The foundations of justice can be traced to the notions of social stability, interdependence, and equality. Ethicist John Rawls feels that the stability of a society depends upon the extent to which its members feel they are being treated justly. When some of society's members come to feel that they are subject to unequal treatment, the foundations have been laid for social unrest, chaos, and strife.

Morality is an extremely important aspect of justice for without morality, the foundations for true justice would cease to exist in a proper manner. Morality has paved the way for a just, decent system that functions solely to ensure that there is a good system of fairness for anything that happens in this world, society and in life, and that the system of justice and fairness is upheld to the best of its ability. It is extremely important that as moral citizens and people that the laws of justice be upheld in an upstanding fair and just manner and without any issues or hesitations. When justice turns into injustice, there can be many varying situations of chaos and unrest and people can riot and not be very happy with what is going on regarding a particular situation or experience.

Chapter 10

Ethical Theories

Right versus wrong. What is true regarding the theories that surround this concept of good versus evil? Is there really a right or wrong and how does this apply to our life and the way we think, behave, and live in general? Morally wrong acts are activities such as murder, theft, rape, lying, and breaking promises. Other descriptions would be that they are morally prohibited, morally impermissible, acts one ought not to do, and acts one has a duty to refrain from doing. Morally right acts are activities that are allowed in a given situation and that don't interfere with creating disharmony, evil consequences, or negative outcomes.

It's difficult to determine sometimes what exactly is right or wrong or what the terms actually mean. Right means something that is correct or it's the way that you should do things. Wrong is something that is not true, incorrect, or something that Is considered to be unjust, immoral, or dishonest. Something that is wrong is something that is going to be unjust or that goes against anything that is good or true, and what is right is something that is correct or that goes for anything that is beneficial, lacking harm, or that is for the benefit of others as a whole.

Theories in moral philosophy help pave the way to better understanding the concepts of right and wrong and allowing us to get a varied perspective on this very concept. Moral philosophy is the branch of learning that deals with the nature of morality and the theories that are used to arrive at decisions about what one ought to do and why. Much has been written about moral philosophy and the theories that support ethical decisions. Ethics or moral philosophy is the philosophical study of moral phenomena. It investigates normative questions about what people ought to do or which behavior is morally right. It is usually divided into three major fields: normative ethics, applied ethics, and metaethics.

Ethics is the study of moral phenomena. It is one of the main branches of philosophy and investigates the nature of morality, and the principles that govern the moral evaluation of conduct, character traits, and institutions. It examines what obligations people have, what behavior is right and wrong, and how to lead a good life.

The terms morality and ethics can be used as the same, but some people draw distinct differences between the two. Morality can be restricted to the question of moral obligations people have, while ethics takes into account what is good or not, or how to lead a more meaningful life. Normative ethics tries to find and justify basic principles of moral conduct. Applied ethics examines the consequences of those principles in domains or areas of practical life. Metaethics is a theory that studies underlying assumptions and concepts, such as what the nature of morality is and what the status of moral judgments are.

Normative Ethics

Normative ethics is the study of ethical conduct and investigates the fundamental principles of morality. Its main goal is to discover and justify general answers to questions such as "how should one live" or "how should a person act?" To do so, it usually seeks universal or domain-independent principles that determine whether an act is right or wrong.

Normative ethics helps and allows people to make moral decisions regarding specific behaviors. Normative ethics mostly describes how people should act during a given time or during a specific scenario or situation. Normative ethics doesn't often ask questions of how ethical beliefs change over time and throughout cultures- those questions are usually asked by other branches of ethics.

Applied Ethics

Applied ethics, also known as practical ethics, is the branch of ethics that examines moral problems encountered in real-life situations. It is not like normative ethics, which is about discovering or justifying universal ethical principles. It studies how those principles can be applied to specific domains of practical life, what effects they have in these fields, and whether other ideas are important regarding the particular area of interest.

Applied ethics covers issues pertaining to both the right conduct in the family and close relationships, and the public sphere, which are moral problems posed by new technologies and international duties toward future generations. There are varying branches that are a part of this and the information they bring forth often overlaps.

Meta Ethics

Meta ethics is the branch of ethics that examines the nature and foundation of moral judgments, concepts, and values. It is not interested in whether actions are right or wrong but in what it means for an action to be right or wrong and whether moral judgments can be true at all. It further examines the meaning of morality and many moral terms. It operates on a higher level of abstraction than normative ethics by investigating its underlying background assumptions. Metaethical theories influence regular theories by questioning the principles on which they were founded and how they are explained.

Metaethics overlaps with various branches of philosophy. Metaethics is mostly concerned with the metaphysical status of moral values and principles. Metaethics discusses whether and how people can acquire moral knowledge.

Metaethics examines basic ethical concepts and their relations. Metaethics covers psychological and anthropological considerations in regard to how moral judgments motivate people to act and how to explain cultural differences in varying moral assessments. It concerns the status of morality and encompasses the question of whether ethical values and principles form a part of reality.

Different ideas within ethical beliefs
Consequentialism

Consequentialism describes an ethical or moral philosophy that describes that which brings about a moral action, brings about desirable consequences. With act consequentialism, decisions and actions which bring about the most desirable consequences are the most moral and those that bring about undesirable consequences are immoral or considered wrong. For example, if backbiting about your significant other could help their self-esteem; in that instance, backbiting may be moral. It's still difficult to know the real outcome of a person's actions though. There may be instances where not committing any of these acts can result in better results for both people. Because of this, act consequentialism depends on the situation itself, and what effects or outcomes the actions of the immoral action can have.

Consequentialism proposes that we can assess whether an action is moral or immoral according to whether the action leads to positive outcomes or not. Lying, for example, tends to lead to negative outcomes. Therefore, according to rule consequentialism speaking truthfully is a moral act, even if it results in an undesirable outcome.

Liberalism

Liberalism is a moral philosophy that emphasizes human freedom. This philosophy was summarized by the nineteenth-century philosopher John Stuart Mill:

"The only purpose for which power can be rightfully exercised over any member of a civilized community, against his will, is to prevent harm to others."

Liberalism is mostly a political moral philosophy that aims to prevent governments from interfering with the lives of people, except for when the actions of people harm others. It is associated with civil libertarianism, a type of political thought that promotes civil liberties (individual freedoms). With this type of belief system, taboo acts such as sex work or drug use can be perceived as acceptable forms of behavior.

Moral Absolutism

Moral absolutism is a belief system that states that there are moral facts and absolute that simply never change. The ten commandments and staunch religious teachings and dogmas present in religious and holy texts are examples of moral absolutism. Stealing is an absolute wrong, along with any of the other beliefs taught, and there is no other means of perceiving the situation. Moral absolutism lacks any concept of flexibility and holds that beliefs and ethical theories, and specific actions are absolute in nature, particularly with regards to the lack of ethics or wrong associated with them. There are many questions that have held philosophers at a stand-still due to the nature of moral absolutism with regards to specific philosophical questions that have been asked throughout time.

Moral Nihilism

Moral nihilism claims that there are no moral facts at all and that there is no basis for any of the teachings regarding morality. Moral nihilism is often associated with moral decay and the downfall of civilization. However, moral nihilism in some way or another finds its way into other moral theories.

Moral Relativism

Moral relativism is a moral philosophy that is nihilistic in nature. It is the view that morality is determined by social convention and is differently understood across cultures and times. According to moral relativists, there is no proper or universal moral code at all. Non-cognitivism states that all of our moral beliefs and foundings are not based on any form of reason, and that they are based on preference and personal taste. If you believe that specific people are moral simply because someone told you they were, it believes you have fallen into a trap of consensus rather than coming up with a rational decision by yourself for your moral beliefs.

It's difficult to know if knowing that there are no moral facts is of benefit to anyone in society out there or if it's a waste to believe in this school of thought. Is there an appropriate way to act? Do morals exist? Moral nihilism says that there are no moral facts, but there may still be non-moral reasons to behave a certain way. Moral nihilism still allows you to live a moral life and believe in specific moral beliefs, without actually defining them as being moral beliefs or actions or ones that are done in the context or right or wrong.

Utilitarianism

Utilitarianism is an ethical theory that determines right from wrong by focusing on outcomes of actions and choices. It holds that the most ethical choice is the one that will have the greatest benefit and produce the greatest good for the most number of people. This is one of the few ways of thinking that actually justifies the military and war. However, we cannot predict the future, and it's difficult to know with certainty whether the consequences of our actions will be good or bad. Utilitarianism is the most reason-based approach to determining the values of right and wrong; however, it has its limitations and there are issues with its school of thought.

Virtue Ethics

Virtue Ethics is a philosophy developed by Aristotle and other Greeks in the quest to understand and live a life of moral character. This is a character-based approach to morality, and it states that we should become virtuous through practice and by being brave, honest, just, generous and by developing moral character. Aristotle felt that if people developed virtuous qualities within themselves, they would make the right choices when faced with moral dilemmas. Virtue ethics helps us understand what it means to be a virtuous human being. It also gives us a guide for living life without giving us specific rules for resolving ethical dilemmas.

Deontology

Deontology is a normative ethical theory that uses rules to distinguish right from wrong. Deontology is often associated with the philosopher Immanuel Kant. Kant believed that ethical actions follow universal moral laws, such as "Don't lie. Don't steal. Don't cheat." According to Kant, morality is affected by rational thought more than by emotion.

Deontology requires that people follow the rules and do their duty. This approach tends to fit well with our natural belief and concepts about what is or isn't ethical. Deontology is unlike consequentialism and doesn't judge actions by their results. This avoids uncertainty because you mostly follow set rules. Deontology states that an act that is not good morally can lead to something good. One example is the act of attacking a thief for trying to steal something, in order to protect everyone from the thief's ill actions. The act of attacking the thief might be wrong; however, if it saves lives and is done in order to prevent a theft, then it is the right thing to do.

Kantian Ethics

Kantian ethics refers to an ethical theory developed by German philosopher Immanuel Kant that is based on the notion that "it is impossible to think of anything at all in the world, or even beyond it that could be good without limitation except a good will." It states that an action can only be moral if it's motivated by a sense of duty and its maxim willed a universal objective law.

The foundation of Kant's system is the doctrine of "transcendental idealism," which emphasizes a distinction between what we can experience (the natural, observable world) and what we cannot (objects such as God and the soul). Kant argued that we can only have knowledge of things we can experience. Kant argues that there are certain moral principles that apply to every situation independent of means-end relations. For Kant, to act morally is to act in accordance with reason as expressed by these principles. He sees immoral actions as irrational by going against the fundamental principles of practical reason.

Kant's ethics are organized around the notion of a "categorical imperative," which is a universal ethical principle stating that one should always respect the humanity in others, and that one should only act in accordance with rules that could hold for everyone. Kant argued that moral law is a truth of reason, and hence that all rational creatures are bound by the same moral law. So in answer to the question, "What should I do?" Kant replies that we should act rationally, in accordance with universal moral law. Kant also argued that his ethical theory requires belief in free will, God, and the immortality of the soul. Belief in the moral law leads to a kind rational faith.

Every school of thought and belief system has their own basis for the teachings they do impart, and various philosophers follow these beliefs and teachings. Both morality and ethics have to do with the concept of right and wrong, and good versus bad, yet the two can be used interchangeably as well. Morality is something that is more of a personal nature pertaining to a specific person or agenda, whereas the concept of ethics has to do with the morals of a specific location, area, or a specific social interaction most of the time.

Ethics can be known as rules of conduct committed in respect to a particular class of human actions or a particular group or culture, whereas morals which are also known for the right and wrong concepts have more to do with a personal compass of that which is right or wrong. Ethics are governed by professional and legal guidelines, within a subset of a time and place, whereas morality transcends cultural norms. Ethics can also be considered a social system or a framework for acceptable behavior. Morals are influenced by culture or society, but they are personal ideations created and upheld by individuals on their own.

It's important to choose wisely and follow a particular school of thought with regards to your own personal beliefs, but also to follow rules and laws that pertain to the greater good of humanity. If you want to live a moral life and live by the true moral code, this is the manner by which you should function on a daily basis, in your daily life and in general. You're able to follow schools of thought that may not hold the most valid and moral theories when it comes to its belief system and teachings, but it's more than likely important that we as souled humans with competent minds follow those teachings that are for the greater good of humanity and of ourselves and of others, and not teachings that stray from this concept or those which teach any form of harm to others or negativity. For that which spreads harm to us or others is the bane of society, and that which needs to be done away with.

What is that which is considered to be good, true and right? Is it that which is moral, or is it that which isn't moral? How can we consider what truly is moral in this world and in society, or are we there to be the judges of that which is good or not good? We can certainly impart our knowledge of that which is true and moral only if we are partaking in that which is truly of the good or that which is beneficial to ourselves and to others.

Ethics are an extremely important part of our lives and everyday worlds for without the concept of ethics or morals, we would find ourselves trapped in a world and culture that lacks civility, decency, and one that would ensue mostly chaos, strife, horror and confusion for all that is in it. We are in dire need of ethics and morals in our culture and society, in order to tame ourselves into becoming the civilized creatures we were meant to be and the manner in which we were always meant to live, which is through the lens of harmony and peace and with happiness, joy and within a culture that is completely awakened, aware and civilized, and not within one that is full of hatred, animosity, chaos, and lack of awareness and goodness.

CHAPTER 11

HOW TO GROW SPIRITUALLY AND MORALLY

"The beauty of spirituality is that it can allow one to grow and flourish morally and allow all that is to bask in the presence and glory of great goodness"

Do you strive to grow as a moral and spiritual person and being, yet find it difficult to do so because of your hectic schedule? Do you find that growing morally seems to be a challenge since you don't have the time or place to think about spiritual or moral ideations or beliefs? You're surely not the only one!

There are many out there who have a hard time with moral growth and becoming familiar with their own personal and moral belief system and even with knowing what their belief system or their ideas or practices are.

There are many various ways to grow spiritually and morally. We need to build on our moral compass and develop habits that allow us to focus on our moral beliefs and our thinking styles and allow us to gain a greater awareness of our own selves in order to develop as strong moral human beings, and to grow morally and spiritually within ourselves. Spirituality and morality can go hand in hand, for gaining a greater increase or boost in your spiritual beliefs in practices can directly affect your moral practices and beliefs as well. Both can go hand in hand and affect each other in a positive way.

There are several core beliefs and methods that allow a person to gain a greater sense of morality within themselves, and which can really allow a person to grow in moral strength and gain a greater spiritual understanding in general and of themselves. Several of these methods are further listed and can allow a person to gain a greater spiritual and moral awareness within and help them grow in various forms as spiritual and moral beings.

Gain a greater awareness of yourself and your beliefs and actions

In order to grow morally, it's important to gain a much greater awareness of your intentions and each and every action that you do in your daily life. Intention is extremely important, and you must have good intent by which you commit your actions. The reason awareness is extremely important is because most people don't have a higher understanding or awareness of the things they are doing in their life or don't have an understanding of the things they partake in regularly and the reason for which they do things. They don't recognize the intent and reasoning behind each and every action they undergo, but once they do, they would fully understand why they commit each action, and it would allow them to gain a greater awareness of their actions thus creating a snowball effect and allowing them to understand more about their beliefs and understandings deep within themselves.

Developing a higher awareness of yourself allows you to further understand and develop as a person and thus allows you to see within yourself the reasoning behind your actions and allows you to further explore your morals and your intention creating a snowball effect of learning more about yourself and expanding your consciousness and increasing your moral levels overall. It's an excellent and great way of doing this.

Pray and focus on peace

In order to grow spiritually and morally it's important to pray regularly or meditate and to focus on your thoughts and actions and really focus on peace, love, joy and harmony. Prayer is an excellent way of increasing your spirituality and even increasing morally in nature. Prayer allows you to sit in deep thought, quietly contemplating and focusing on God and allowing yourself to become immersed in contemplation and lack of thought, and only on pleasing and becoming close to the Creator.

Prayer is of excellent benefit as it raises your spiritual levels, raises your vibration overall and increases your level of morality. It allows you to gain a greater peace within yourself, your mind, and allows you to become immersed in goodness, light, and love. The closer you become to God and the more you meditate or pray and sit in quiet contemplation, the greater your chances are of becoming a more moral person, because you will follow the teachings of the belief or religious system you are practicing through, and it will allow your moral compassion to come through and increase and become elevated.

Gaining a greater sense of peace allows one to gain an inner harmony and lets you be one with yourself, and just lets you be the person that you seek to be. Quiet contemplation such as prayer allows those meditative practices to let you gain a greater sense of peace within, and increases your levels of morality and spirituality, and lets your awareness grow so you can ponder upon life's questions, and deal with your own inner issues. You become a stronger and more spiritual person within and are able to grow your levels of morality and spiritual guises as well.

Increase your empathy and compassion

Empathy and compassion are the gateways to greater spirituality and morality. Empathy is the gateway to becoming a more humble, kind, happy individual and allowing one to cultivate harmony and joy within a person's self. Empathy is the concept of caring about someone else, and putting yourself in another person's situation or shoes, and putting yourself in other people's situation with compassion and goodness allows you to become a more spiritual and moral person overall. It will increase your morality and goodness and especially your spiritual levels as well. Compassion is the gateway to goodness, harmony, humbleness, and allows you to grow morally and spiritually as well.

These qualities allow you to understand and appreciate the emotions of others, which allows you to make more ethical decisions and live a moral life. To increase empathy and compassion, practice active listening, be active in your communities, help others and volunteer, and take the time to do what you can to become a better person.

Educate yourself on ethical theories and philosophies

In order to grow morally and spiritually it's key that you educate yourself on the many ethical theories and philosophies that are out there with regards to morality and even with spirituality. Once you educate yourself with these theories, you'll gain a greater understanding of the various concepts of morality and spirituality, and your moral understanding will increase so will your spiritual levels. This provides you with a framework of ethical decision making and allows you to deepen your understanding overall of these very concepts.

Read books, attend lectures, or participate in discussions on ethics and morality to deepen your understanding of these concepts.

Take responsibility for your actions

It's important to take responsibility for your actions and learn from your mistakes. Doing so is essential to gaining a greater understanding of yourself and growing spiritually and morally as well. When you make a mistake or realize that your decision has negatively impacted others, acknowledge it, apologize, and learn from the experience. Reflect on what you could have done differently and commit to making better choices in the future. Taking responsibility for your actions constitutes being able to make greater ethical decisions in your life and in the future.

Taking responsibility for your actions allows you to further ponder upon the many scenarios that are taking place in your life and allows you to psychoanalyze the deeper aspects happening to yourself. It also lets you think upon these scenarios and allows you to grow as a human being and as a spiritual and moral person. The more questions you ask with regards to your actions and behaviors, and the more you analyze and contemplate these scenarios, the greater your level of spiritual understanding will be and the greater the level your moral growth will take place. You will grow morally as a person and begin to understand more and ethically will begin to want to make the right choices and decisions for you will have gained a grander awareness of all these processes that have been taking place.

Growing morally and spiritually takes time and is not something that happens overnight. It is not something that is done on a whim. If you want to grow spiritually or morally, you will have to focus on the good aspects in your life and do away with all the negative aspects, and only then will you be able to raise your vibration and harness your focus on that which is spiritual and positive. In order to be a moral and spiritual person, you will need to cultivate and practice extreme amounts of empathy, kindness, and compassion.

Developing a strong sense of morality is a lifelong journey that involves self-reflection, learning, and practice. By following these steps regularly, you can strengthen your moral values and your spiritual life and ideations and further reflect on your core values and increase them in a great way and make decisions with greater ethical values. Remember that growth is an ongoing process, and striving to improve your ethical decision-making will lead to a more fulfilling and responsible life. Embrace self-reflection, learn from your experiences. Engage in open-minded discussions, challenge your beliefs, and stay informed about ethical issues. By nurturing empathy, practicing active listening, and growing your moral and spiritual awareness you can contribute to the world in a positive and beneficial way.

Modern moral values and teachings are being researched and analyzed and are being brought into fruition through different means. Ethics and morals are the way by which we live our daily lives and how we perceive varying values through the lens of our own moral understanding. We hope to aim and strive towards doing that which is honest, ethical, and of good faith and integrity as opposed to committing actions that may not be moral in nature. That which is immoral or against morality isn't going to be the best option to do what is for the greater good of humanity and of nature in general.